A guide to the historic sites and buildings along eight miles of the Aire Valley through Leeds

by
Peter Brears
Director, Leeds City Museum

Leeds City Museums in association with
Leeds Waterfront TDAP
1993

ISBN 0 907588 08 5

In association with Leeds Waterfront TDAP

Published by: Leeds City Museums

Typeset by: West Yorkshire Archaeology Service

Printed by: The Alden Press, Oxford

Cover photograph: The Leeds Waterfront, looking downstream from Victoria Bridge

Inset photograph on fold-out: The Leeds Waterfront, Victoria Bridge

CONTENTS

NOTE

The trail passes through some relatively isolated locations. Walkers who might be concerned about this may prefer to follow the trail in the company of a few friends.

INTRODUCTION

Welcome to the Leeds Waterfront Heritage Trail!

The Leeds Waterfront is one of Europe's most surprising and interesting historic landscapes. For centuries its waterways enabled Leeds to develop and prosper as England's northern capital, the River Aire powering its mills, the Aire and Calder Navigation bringing in coal and raw materials, and exporting manufactured goods to Europe, and the Leeds and Liverpool Canal carrying Leeds' products across the Pennines for export to the Americas, Asia and the expanding Empire.

As Leeds rose to become one of *the* great workshops of the world, its factories produced vast amounts of smoke and effluent which turned both the air and the river water a sooty black. Then, as heavy industry went into decline, it left behind dereliction and decay. This was very evident in the 1960s and '70s, but since then an amazing transformation has taken place. New buildings and bridges have been erected, old buildings have been cleaned, restored and imaginatively converted to new uses, and areas of dereliction sensitively landscaped. Through these activities, hundreds of people have moved into riverside homes, new hotels, restaurants, shops and offices have developed, and the whole environment improved beyond recognition. Leeds has been declared Environment City of the United Kingdom. Now visitors from all parts of Yorkshire, Britain and overseas can appreciate its numerous attractions. They include lush woodland, a great medieval abbey, a wealth of industrial archaeology, fascinating museums, craft shops, pubs and restaurants, and lively shopping areas, all linked by the eight-mile Leeds Waterfront Heritage Trail.

In order to promote the public use, enjoyment and appreciation of this fine historic environment, the Leeds Waterfront Tourist Development Action Programme was established in 1990. Over the past three years its partners, Leeds City Council, British Waterways, Leeds Development Corporation and the English and Yorkshire Tourist Boards, have made considerable progress, making thousands of people aware of the Waterfront and its varied attractions. Their success in establishing the Heritage Trail has also been greatly enhanced by the assistance of Leeds City Council's Planning and Cultural Services committees, the National Rivers Authority, and the Leeds/Bradford City Action Team. Together they have sponsored the necessary waymarking and interpretation, in addition to providing funding towards the erection of a new footbridge across the river at Knostrop. Little of this would have been achieved, however, without the skilful co-ordination provided by Leeds Waterfront's Director, Mr Don Waterman and the knowledge and commitment of Peter Brears, Director of Museums.

We hope that you will visit the Trail, either on foot, by road or on the waterways, and see for yourself what it has to offer. Two things should be remembered, one is that the Leeds Waterfront is not preserved in aspic, for it still continues to develop and improve. Tetley's Brewery Wharf and the new Tower Armouries are expected to bring at least a million new visitors here every year, and additional visitor facilities will undoubtedly follow their impressive lead. The other is that both Leeds City Council and the Leeds Chamber of Commerce and Industry, while celebrating our industrial heritage, are determined to preserve the existing manufacturing industry in Leeds, and to retain the position of Leeds as a major industrial city as well as one renowned for its financial, economic and legal significance.

John D. Jackson, CBE
Chairman, Leeds Waterfront

Bernard Atha, OBE
Chairman, Cultural Services Committee, Leeds City Council

THE LEEDS WATERFRONT

A BRIEF HISTORY

Before exploring the Leeds Waterfront, it is worthwhile to learn something of its past, so that its individual features can be seen as part of a long story of development and change. Only in this way can we appreciate why Leeds came to be built here, and why its waterways were made to carry merchandise to and from virtually every part of the world.

At the most basic level, Leeds owes its success to the raw materials which were deposited here millions of years ago, particularly during the Carboniferous period. Its range of Lower Coal Measure deposits include rough rocks and sandstones ideal for building work, clays for pottery and brickmaking, ironstone for making iron, and rich seams of coal to fuel both factories and homes. In addition, its soft water was ideal for the wool textile industry, while the limestones available just a short distance to the east were useful for industry and agriculture.

The Aire valley itself received its present shape in the Ice Age, when massive glaciers carved deep channels through the underlying rocks as they slowly moved eastwards towards the North Sea. During one of the warm interglacial periods around 124,000 BC mammals first became evident here, the bones of hippopotamus and straight-tusked elephant being found at Armley, and sections of massive mammoth tusk in the gravels below Thwaite Mills. This was a period of major erosion, when the valley downstream was deepened by some 30 metres.

After the last glaciation, between 60,000 and 12,000 BC, the Leeds area was left with additional economic advantages, for not only did it have a river valley ideal for exploiting water power, but it also lay in a uniquely advantageous position for future trade. To the west, the Aire Gap provided the easiest crossing of the Pennine hills anywhere between Derbyshire and the Scottish border, while a glacial moraine, a long raised ridge running above the boggy plains from Tadcaster to York, effectively continued this trade route across the entire country through to the east coast. In addition, Leeds lay in the best position for the country's main north-south route, avoiding both the low, wet lands to the east, and the steep-sided valleys to the west, while yet providing firm bases for fords and bridges at major river crossings. In the medieval period this route linked a string of major churches, market towns, castles and bridges, often with accompanying chapels, which extended from the south, through Derby and along the A61 up to Ripon and the North, close to the line of the present M1.

This is the tusk of a mammoth that lived in the Leeds area some 38,600 years ago. It was found at Newsam Green, downstream from Thwaite Mills.

The first evidence of human activity in this area comes from Thorpe Stapleton, some four miles east of Leeds, where a group of people living off the land by hunting and gathering wild fruits etc. settled around 6,000 BC. By 3,500 BC family groups moving here from Europe had introduced domestic animals and seed-corn, which enabled them to start farming. Some of their beautifully polished stone axes probably came along the Aire Gap trade route from Langdale, in the Lake District. Around 2,000 BC the manufacture and use of copper tools was introduced from Europe, and people began to bury their dead with fine hand-made pottery vessels, one being found in Briggate in 1745. Soon the copper tools were being replaced by those of bronze, these being supplemented from the 7th century BC by much harder and tougher ones made of iron. The Brigantes, the local confederation of Iron Age tribes began to establish small farming settlements of round timber huts in this area, some of which have been excavated at Dalton Parlours near Collingham. During troublesome periods they retreated to strongly defended hill-forts, one probably overlooking the valley from Rampart Road, on Woodhouse Moor.

From the middle of the 1st century AD, *Brigantia* came under increasing Roman influence, the Romans probably building a camp on Quarry Hill called *Campodunum*, its banks and ditches, and the place-name 'Campo' both surviving well into the 19th

The Leeds Cross in the parish church was probably carved as a grave marker in the late 9th-early 10th centuries. It features a mixture of both mythological and Christian motifs.

century. It is possible that the Romans also established a river crossing near Leeds Bridge, and various finds of Roman altars, coins, pottery etc. have been made in the Leeds area.

After the Romans left, around AD 400, an estate corresponding to the medieval parish of Leeds appears to have formed part of the British kingdom of Elmet, later becoming part of the Anglo-Saxon kingdom of Northumbria in 617. There is evidence that King Edwin then set up a royal house here in 'Loidis', and that Paulinus built the town's first wooden church (predecessor of the present Leeds Parish Church) which was burnt down in 633 by Penda, King of Mercia. After the battle of Winwaed in 654 this area returned to Northumbria, becoming part of the Viking kingdom of York after the great Danish victory of 867. Viking names were very evident here in 1066, when lands along the trail were held by Morfari, Arnetill, Thorsteinn and other thegns.

After the Norman conquest, Leeds was granted to the de Lacy family, forming part of their Honor of Pontefract. By this time the area had been divided into separate administrative and agricultural units, the townships or vills of Bramley, Armley, Headingley, Beeston, Hunslet and Leeds itself, each controlled by its own sub-tenant. Over the course of the following centuries, the parish church was rebuilt, large earthwork castles were established at Leeds and Armley, the abbey at Kirkstall and the preceptory of the Knights Templar at Temple Newsam were founded, and a new borough of Leeds, still recognisable as Briggate and its adjoining yards, was set up in 1207. Industrial activity flourished too. There had been a single corn mill in Leeds in 1086, but by 1185 the first recorded fulling mill in England was working at Temple Newsam, mechanising a laborious but essential cloth-finishing process. In the 14th century Leeds had a coal mine, a forge, weavers, dyers and a water-powered fulling mill. The late 15th and early 16th century saw this infant textile industry flourish rapidly, as the good supplies of wool, cheap food and labour, and freedom from guild restrictions, enabled Leeds and the other West Riding towns to capture the trade of the old textile centres of York and Beverley.

The Dissolution of the monasteries in 1539 gave a great boost to the local economy, since it released large areas of land for potential agricultural and industrial use. Within a short time new fulling mills had been built at Armley Mills and Thwaite Mills, an iron forge established at Kirkstall and a glass furnace set up in Hawksworth Woods, while the Abbey's own corn mills and maltings went into private ownership. These activities did little to harm the rural peace of the Aire valley, which remained as beautiful as ever, with its narrow strip of riverside pastures set between the wooded bluffs of the Bank, Armley, Bramley Fall and Hawksworth. Around 1600 Michael Drayton celebrated the river in his *Polyolbion*:

> '*Now speak I of a flood who thinks there's none should dare*
> *Once to compare her, suppos'd by her descent*
> *The darling daughter born of lofty Penigent*
> *Who from her father's foot, by Skipton down doth scud,*
> *And leading thence to Leeds, that delicatest flood*
> *Takes Calder coming in by Wakefield ......*'

Now handloom weavers from the bleak hills to the west brought even more fulled but otherwise unfinished cloths for sale to the merchants at Leeds market, then using the money they had received to buy food which had been brought into the market from the fertile plains to the east. The merchants went on to complete the important processes of dyeing, dressing and cropping the cloth, before arranging for its sale either to travelling salesmen, to merchants attending the London markets, or to agents and merchants overseas. This extremely profitable trade enabled one Leeds merchant, John Harrison, to rebuild the town's 1552 grammar school in 1624, erect St John's Church in 1634, build almshouses and a new street, and undertake numerous charitable works. In 1626 the importance of Leeds was recognised by the granting of its first charter as a municipal borough, with special responsibilities for regulating the cloth trade. Despite problems caused by the Civil War and plague, this prosperity continued to grow, a new charter of 1661 giving Leeds a mayor, aldermen and

This engraving of Leeds by William Lodge shows the cloth drying on the tenter-frames by the riverside. The cloth market is taking place on the original Leeds Bridge, where it was held, up to 14th June 1684.

councillors, and the right to hold quarter session courts. In addition, the merchants finally overcame centuries of opposition from York by obtaining parliament's consent in 1699 to construct the Aire and Calder Navigation, establishing Leeds as a major inland port, with direct links to the London, Low Countries and Baltic trade through the Humber and the port of Hull. Up to this time Leeds merchants had had to send their cloth by road to the nearest wharfs at Rawcliffe, Goole or Selby 'having no conveniency of water carriage within sixteen miles of them, which not only occasions great expence, but many times great damage to their goods, and sometimes the roads are impassable'. By clearing a number of obstacles, and building a lock at the side of

The Aire and Calder Navigation, as it appears in Sutton Nicholls' map of 1712. The oval enclosures are the principal parks and landed estates in the Aire valley.

Leeds Dam, these problems were now solved. From November 1700 boats could sail up to Leeds Bridge, where a new Town's Warehouse had been erected on the northern bank.

During the 18th century, Leeds flourished as the centre of the great international wool-textile trade. This was conducted through the cloth halls, successively larger ones for white cloth being built in 1711, 1756, and 1775, and one for coloured cloth in 1758, thus creating almost 3,000 stalls where the handloom weavers could display their cloth to the merchants at the Tuesday and Saturday markets. The vast profits made by the merchants, as they exported the finished wares to virtually every part of the known world, were used to promote the town's social and economic life. By the 1790s, it had all the facilities required for an elegant Georgian life-style, with assembly rooms, theatre, concert hall, music hall, subscription library and local newspapers as well as fine new churches, Non-Conformist and Roman Catholic chapels, and one of Britain's finest hospitals. A host of skilled craftsmen and shopkeepers supplied luxuries for the wealthy merchant class, while the tablewares made in the Leeds Pottery served both local and international markets. Investment in the construction of turnpike roads now provided efficient coaching and haulage services, but the town's economic life was still dependent on its waterways.

One of the main problems of using the natural course of the river for navigation was its uncertain flow, particularly since it was liable to major floods following heavy rains in Leeds or further upstream. In August 1767, it rose over six feet in a single hour, while a 36-hour deluge in October 1775 left the whole riverside under water: 'large quantities of grain deposited in warehouses were washed away, cloth in some places torn from the tenters, in others the cloth and tenters were carried away together; several dwelling houses and dye-houses suffered greatly, dyeing vats being torn out of their places; the pavement in the streets broken up; walls thrown down; cows, horses and sheep forced into the water and drowned'. Lesser floods were still troublesome, particularly for vessels proceeding up to Leeds. By a further Act of 1774, new navigable channels were cut alongside the river at Knostrop and Thwaite, a mile or more downstream, thus greatly improving the passage of vessels up and down the Navigation.

As Leeds' export trade expanded, there was an increasing need for an efficient means of transporting goods across the Pennines to Liverpool, and on to America and other distant markets. Following a survey carried out by John Longbottom of Halifax, an Act of Parliament was obtained in May 1770 to build a canal from Leeds to Liverpool. Construction commenced that year, following an improved course designed by James Brindley and Robert Whitworth. As Joseph Priestley, the Aire and Calder Navigation's chief clerk stated, this was 'one of the boldest and most magnificent projects hitherto attempted in Great Britain. Indeed contemporaries marvelled at the length of the

This patriotic cartouche, featuring a Leeds weaver, the Golden Fleece, and an Aire and Calder Navigation boat, was printed on a Leeds Pottery mug in the late 18th century.

canal, but much more awesome was the mountainous landscape which had to be negotiated between the two towns. The difference in water levels at Leeds Bridge and the canal basin at North Lady's Walk in Liverpool was a mere 21 feet but in its eventual course of 127 miles the canal climbed 411 feet over undulating terrain necessitating 844 feet of lockage, 8 aquaducts, a massive embankment two-thirds of a mile long, and over one-and-a-quarter miles of tunnel'. Construction started at both ends, the section up to Gargrave, just beyond Skipton, being completed by 1777. Then, as the *Leeds Intelligencer* reported, 'this noble and grand undertaking now affords the most safe, easy, cheap and expeditious method of conveying the produce of different countries to and from the populous manufacturing towns ... Its execution hath given employment and bread to the indigent and laborious; drawn forth latent merit; raised genius from obscurity and improved and advanced Agriculture and the Arts of the extensive and populous parts through which it passes and which it ornaments and adorns'. The entire route was not completed until 1816, when vessels could finally cross from Leeds to Liverpool in the course of a single journey.

While the waterways were being improved a major transformation had taken place in the economy of Leeds. The merchants now began to take over the manufacturing processes by building large factories equipped with the most modern machinery. Thomas Lloyd had started this process by rebuilding Armley Mills in 1788-90, but the

The close association between the waterways and the major industrial areas of Leeds, is clearly illustrated in this birds-eye view looking upstream through Leeds in 1893.

greatest advance took place in 1792 when Benjamin Gott built the world's first major integrated woollen mill at Bean Ing, on the River Aire just upstream from Leeds. Similarly, in 1791 John Marshall and Thomas Benyon started the first mechanised flax-spinning mill in Holbeck, using machinery made by Marshall's mechanic, Matthew Murray. As the demand for steam-engines, factory machinery and machine tools increased, Murray and his partners Fenton and Wood established the Round Foundry in Water Lane, Holbeck, in 1797. Here his skill and ingenuity produced a remarkable series of practical inventions, which excited the jealousy and 'dirty tricks' of Boulton and Watt of Birmingham. Improved beam engines, new forms of valve, steam-powered boats, hydraulic presses, and the design and construction of the world's first practical steam railway locomotive were among his many achievements. From this inspired beginning, Leeds developed as one of the world's great centres of engineering, virtually the whole town, south of the river, being devoted to the industry.

During the early 19th century the Leeds waterways flourished, as vast tonnages of raw materials and finished products moved in and out of the town. Incoming barges brought coal to power factories and heat homes, stone, slate and marble for building works, limestone and iron-ore for iron and steel works, flint and clay for the potteries, corn for milling into flour or animal food, flax and wool for the textile industry, seeds for crushing into oils, milling into mustard, or processing into cattle food, hides for leather, and timber for buildings, for construction carriages, furniture etc. and for making dyestuffs. Outgoing barges were loaded with coal, slate and stone, a wealth of engineering products, leather, cloth and numerous other Leeds-made items.

As the town mushroomed, new factories began to line the riverbanks; iron forges, engineering factories, textile mills, chemical works, dyehouses, oil mills, grinding mills, saw mills, corn mills, tanneries etc. many of which used the waterways both as a means of transport, and as a convenient, if unhygienic, drain and sewer. Up to the mid-19th century, the river still had fish in abundance, as may be seen in the following note by the Joy family of Thwaite Mills.

'May 1834, Drew the leap [basket trap] breakfast time, 8-stone fish; dinnertime, 10-stone fish; 50 stone within last few days'

These were soon to disappear, however, poisoned by the dyes, chemicals and other effluent which poured into the Aire. Leeds now developed an unenviable reputation as one of the most polluted towns in Europe, virtually every visitor being repelled by its foul water, and foul air.

In 1843 T.J. Maslen described how the river banks 'are crowded and shut up with buildings, and its waters are like a reservoir of poison, carefully kept for the purpose of breeding a pestilence in the town. In that part of the river, extending from Armley Mills to King's Mills, it is charged with the drainage and contents of about two hundred water- closets, cesspools and privies, a great number of common drains, the drainings of dung-hills, the infirmary (dead leeches, poultices for patients etc), slaughter houses, chemical, soap, gas, drug, dye-houses and manufacturers, spent blue and black dye, pig manure, old urine wash, with all sorts of dead animal and vegetable substances, and now and then a decomposed human body; forming an annual mass of filth equal to thirty million gallons! This was, until lately, the delicious nectar, the delectable water that went to make tea to be carried to the lips of the beautiful young ladies of Leeds'.

The construction of the first sewerage system in Leeds from the early 1850s slightly improved the situation in the town centre, by collecting the raw effluent and dumping it into the river a couple of miles downstream near Knostrop. Even so, William Osburn's poetic description of Leeds written in 1857 was just as relevant a century later:

'The AIRE below is doubly dyed and damned;
The AIR above, with lurid smoke is crammed:
The ONE flows steaming foul as Charon's Styx,
Its poisonous vapours in the other mix.

These sable twins the murky town invest -
By them the skin's begrimed, the lungs oppressed.
How dear the penalty thus paid for wealth,
Obtained through wasted life and broken health....'

Although the waterways continued to play a major role in the continuing expansion of Leeds' manufacturing industries, their virtual monopoly began to be eroded in the early 19th century, when major new turnpike road works were undertaken on the Leeds and Bradford and the Kirkstall, Ilkley and Shipley routes. Access across the valley was further improved by building new bridges at Whitehall Road in 1818-19, Newlay in 1819, Monk Bridge in 1827, South Accommodation Road in 1828 and Crown Point in 1840-42. As traffic increased, new and larger bridges then had to be built at Leeds Bridge in 1871-3, Canal Road in 1882, Monk Bridge in 1886, South Accommodation Road in 1898, and Kirkstall in 1912. Of greater significance, however, was the expansion of the railways in the mid 1840s, when the Leeds and Bradford and Leeds and Thirsk lines were built alongside sections of the Leeds and Liverpool Canal.

This photograph of around 1900 presents a vivid picture of the River Aire at its junction with the Leeds and Liverpool Canal. Note the steam tug on the left, the steam cranes unloading coal boats on the right, and the boats under construction across the river.

These were followed in 1866-9 by the construction of the New Station and its accompanying viaduct, which sliced through the town centre just north of the river, forming a permanent and virtually impenetrable barrier between Leeds and its waterfront. In addition, many of the larger factories then improved their transport facilities by constructing branch lines, which enabled them to move their products around their extensive sites, and then directly onto the nation-wide railway system.

Despite this competition, the waterways still continued to be extremely busy, the early 19th-century expansion of the docks and warehouses, together with the rebuilding of the Navigation's locks, enabling vast tonnages to be handled each year. As Tom Bradley observed in 1893, 'If we stand on the Suspension Bridge at Hunslet or the Crown Point Bridge and look upon the number of vessels moored at the wharfs discharging their cargoes or being trawled along the inky stream by the powerful steam tugs, we gain some slight idea of the advantages of the river as a means of carriage and the amount of traffic that passes into the port of Leeds.' By now the waterways were mainly used for heavy, bulky cargoes such as coal, stone, sand, chalk, timber, hides, grain and potatoes. These remained the mainstay of the Navigation and the Canal through into the 20th century, the importance of coal increasing considerably with the opening of power stations at Crown Point, Whitehall Road, and Kirkstall. From the 1920s, there was a noticeable decline in some of Leeds' traditional heavy industries, Clarence Ironworks closing in 1921, and Leeds Forge in 1936, for example, similar closures continuing through the 40s, 50s and 60s. The construction of British Waterways new depot at Knostrop in the 1950s, the development of oil and petrol stores nearby, and the mechanisation of the locks has ensured that the Aire and Calder Navigation continues to operate successfully today, but commercial traffic on the Leeds and Liverpool Canal had virtually ceased by 1970.

Following the decline in the commercial use of the waterways, they tended to be forgotten by most Leeds people, but from the late 1970s their potential for recreation and tourism slowly began to emerge. On the face of things, it was still a distinctly uninspiring prospect, many of the waterside buildings being in a semi-derelict state, the towpaths almost completely overgrown in places, and its finest features, such as the bridges and viaducts, still stained jet black by industrial pollution.

Since then, there have been many notable improvements to the Leeds Waterfront. British Waterways have invested around £1 million in improvements and conservation works for example, their excellent standards of maintenance being recognised by national awards. They have also mounted joint ventures with other organisations such as the City Council and the Leeds Development Corporation to enhance the Waterfront environment. Private development has also played a major part in this process, firstly by transforming the Dark Arches, the dank, gloomy and distinctly unsavoury vaults beneath the City Station, into Granary Wharf, a bright, lively and interesting area where thousands come every weekend to enjoy the craft markets, cafés and live entertainments. This was followed by a whole series of major Waterfront developments in the City centre, where the best of the old properties have been refurbished to the highest standards, and the worst ones demolished so that their sites could be sensitively rebuilt using traditional local materials. As a result, the Waterfront now has an excellent range of office buildings, shops, hotels, restaurants and, perhaps most important of all, attractive homes for people who can now live in the centre of Leeds. These dramatic changes have enabled the central area of the Waterfront to serve Leeds' expanding role as the major British legal, financial and economic centre outside London.

The recreational use of the Waterfront has also been greatly improved, most lengths of the towpath having been cleared and resurfaced for the benefit of walkers, joggers, and the local angling clubs who lease the fishing rights. Far more privately owned and hire boats now use the waterways, while the Kirkstall Flyboat carries thousands of people in groups from its base in the canal basin.

In addition the quality of some sections of the Waterfront has been recognised by their nomination as conservation areas, since their special historical and architectural interest and character makes them worthy of preservation and enhancement. Similarly many of its buildings and a number of the locks have been protected by being given 'listed' status. In 1984 the section of canal running from Rodley down to Armley Mills was designated as a Site of Special Scientific Interest, since the low levels of pollution and turbidity, combined with an alkaline water supply and a base of rich puddled clay provide the best example of a slow-flowing fresh-water habitat in the county. Its rich flora includes scarce pondweeds, arrowhead, rush, flag and mosses, while pike, roach, gudgeon, frogs, toads and freshwater molluscs thrive here.

Now the value of the Waterfront both to visitors and to the people of Leeds and its region is fully appreciated. British Waterways, the City Council, the Leeds Development Corporation, the English and Yorkshire Tourist Boards all help to enhance and promote it, both through their individual initiatives, and through their combined activities in the Leeds Waterfront Tourist Development Action Programme. The voluntary sector also plays a very active part in determining the future of the river corridor by expressing the views of its residents, and organising appropriate events. It is largely represented by Eye on the Aire, an umbrella body of 30 voluntary organisations affiliated to important organisations and firms from the public and private sector.

The first major initiative to develop the recreational, educational and tourist potential of the Leeds Waterfront was undertaken by the City Museums in 1982, when, with the active help of British Waterways, it established a Museum of Leeds Trail which linked three major museums with 40 historic sites along the Leeds and Liverpool towpath. Following its opening by B.B.C's *Blue Peter* team, it rapidly won national and European recognition in the Museum of the Year Awards. Its judges praised 'The ambitious purpose of this much enlarged museum concept to interpret the development of the entire Leeds district over the past millennium to local residents, in addition to providing a major regional leisure and tourist attraction. It is one of the handful of really imaginative and influential museums to have been created in Europe during the past thirty years'. Since then, the City Museums have greatly expanded Armley Mills Museum, undertaken major conservation work at Kirkstall Abbey, taken over Thwaite Mills Museum, and combined its resources with Leeds Waterfront TDAP to establish this Heritage Trail.

By the early 1990s, over 200,000 visitors were coming to see the museums and other historic sites along the Trail, but this was just a beginning, as greater numbers will be drawn to the Leeds Waterfront to visit Tetley's Brewery Wharf, the Royal Armouries, and the City's numerous other attractions.

THE LEEDS WATERFRONT HERITAGE TRAIL

The trail starts $5\frac{1}{2}$ miles north-west of Leeds, in the village of Rodley, and follows the course of the Leeds and Liverpool Canal and the Aire and Calder Navigation down the Aire valley, through Leeds, to Thwaite Mills, $1\frac{1}{2}$ miles south-east of the city. Most of this distance is followed on footpaths, linked by only short stretches of road. It is quite possible to walk the whole length, including the offshoots to Newlay Bridge and Kirkstall Abbey in a single day, but this would give very little time to appreciate the many fine buildings, museums and open spaces along the way. Using public transport, it can easily be split up into a number of easy sections, leaving or joining buses at Rodley, Newlay, Kirkstall, Armley, the city centre, or Thwaite Gate. Alternatively its major attractions can be visited by car, good parking being available at Kirkstall Abbey, Armley Mills, Granary Wharf and Thwaite Mills.

It should be remembered that the trail, whether in the rural suburbs, or in the inner city, passes through some relatively isolated locations. Walkers who might be concerned about this may prefer to follow the trail in the company of a few friends.

Please note that, with the exception of the route marked on the maps, and those museums, inns, shopping areas, parks and woodlands etc. obviously open to the public, the remainder of the features described in the Waterfront Heritage Trail are all private property, with no right of access.

For ease of reference, this guide assumes that the river and canal run from west to east with various features lying on their northern and southern banks.

Walking the trail at Oddy's Lock.

THE WATERFRONT HERITAGE TRAIL

Rodley: the canalside cottages.

Although the towpath and dock areas are the private property of British Waterways and other owners, the public are invited to visit them in order to follow this trail. Lying on the Leeds and Liverpool Canal, and just within the Leeds Ring Road, Rodley makes an ideal starting point for the trail. It is on good bus routes, has a range of public houses, take-aways and shops, a public phone-box, and public conveniences on the main road, close to the Owl Hotel.

In the 18th century this was a tiny hamlet, with a few cottages where the Calverley-Bramley road crossed Bagley Beck. With the coming of the canal in the 1770s, and the development of its engineering works, Rodley grew into a self-contained village of late Georgian and Victorian houses, complete with churches, chapels, schools and a recreation ground.

To start the trail, walk down Canal Road, past the Barge Inn, to the raised stone wharf, the base of a warehouse where goods were loaded and unloaded from the barges, then cross the swing bridge, join the Leeds and Liverpool Canal towpath, and walk downstream, to the right.

1. RODLEY FOLD

The farm seen across the nearby fields is the sole surviving section of Rodley Fold, a group of 17th-18th-century cottages largely demolished in the 1950s. Their water supply came from a single iron pump, while for timekeeping one cottage had a sundial inscribed 'This plainly shows to foolish man That his whole life is but a span'.

While following the towpath, note the quarter, half and mile-posts, the latter having plaques recording the distances to Leeds and to Liverpool. They date from the 1890s.

2. THE CRANE WORKS

Rodley was a major centre of the crane-building industry, enjoying a world-wide reputation for its products. In 1820 Messrs Smith, Balmforth and Booth established their workshops here for the manufacture of equipment for woollen mills, gas fittings and the winches and cutting machines required in the local gritstone quarries.

During 1847 Joseph Booth left the partnership, and began making cranes at his own factory on this site, cranes of all types being built, one of the late 19th-century developments being the steam-powered overhead crane. In 1901 the firm began to make its own electric

The girder shop at Joseph Booth's Union Crane works at Rodley, around 1930. From the stockyard in the distance, the girders proceeded forward through the cutting off, setting out and machine bays, to the assembly bay in the foreground. The raised floor on the left was where templates were prepared.

crane motors, going on to produce steam, electric or diesel-powered cranes for docks, workshops, steelworks and railways. During the First World War breach blocks, mines and depth charges were made in large quantities, but when peace returned the company introduced battery-operated locomotives and trucks, for mines and factories, to its range of cranes.

William Balmforth also left the partnership in 1863, to concentrate on making quarry cranes, his first steam crane excavator appearing in 1887. The firm left its Peel Ings Foundry in Rodley in 1916 for new premises in Bath Lane, Bramley.

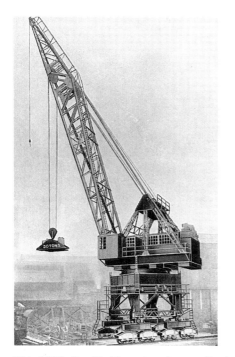

This 1930s Booth's 30-ton portal crane, fitted with an auxiliary whip hoist, was particularly suitable for use in dry docks.

Thomas Smith, the remaining partner, continued to manufacture cranes, the small hand-powered models of the 1840s being succeeded in the 1860s by steam cranes, followed by railway cranes in 1880, steam excavators in 1887, and electric cranes in 1902. From that time the company made cranes suitable for the most demanding situations, their plant being used in numerous important projects, including the Manchester Ship Canal, Mersey Docks, King George V Dock, Southampton, the Egyptian and Sudanese barrages at Aswan Assiout and Nag Hamadi, Singapore Naval Base, and the Victoria Falls and Zambesi River Bridges. Similarly they adopted the most advanced crane building techniques as they became available, from caterpillar tracks in the First World War, to hydraulic cranes in 1965.

In 1978 Thomas Smith & Sons (Rodley) Ltd was incorporated with Clyde Booth, successors of its former partners, to form part of the unified NEI Cranes group. Recently the downstream end of the works has been demolished, its place being taken by an attractive modern housing scheme. In 1993 Rodley Engineering, which now occupies part of the site, built a number of swing bridges for roads crossing the canal.

3. AIREDALE MILLS

These scribbling and fulling mills were built by a combination of 20 small manufacturers who met at the Fleece Inn, Farsley, in 1860, to set up the Airedale Mill Company. It then continued to provide accommodation for a number of woollen manufacturers, who were joined in the 1930s by dyers, oil

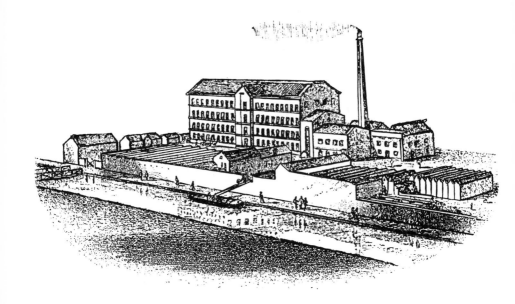

Airedale Mills in 1893. Note the man with a wheelbarrow loading a bale of cloth from the top of the factory wall directly onto a barge.

extractors etc. It is currently occupied by George Barker & Co. (Leeds) Ltd.

4. ROSS MILLS

The first mills here on the bank of the River Aire were probably built before the 13th century, when Adam de Reineville granted *de molendino de Bramley,* or mills at Bramley, to Kirkstall Abbey. By 1808 they were being worked by James Hudson for scribbling and fulling. He suffered damage estimated at £4,000 when they burnt down in 1829. From the mid-19th century James Stead operated the mills, suffering a similar fire in 1866, while William Pearson & Co., who took over the mills in 1910, finally abandoned the riverside site following a further fire in 1914. The company then built new spinning sheds at the opposite side of the canal, where it had built its weaving sheds some years earlier.

5. WHITECOTE HOUSE

Built in the early 19th century, this house was later occupied by a number of different families, including those of William Nichols, maltster, in the 1860s, and Lemuel Westcott, colliery agent, in the 1890s.

6. FALLWOOD MARINA

Now used as long-term moorings for leisure craft on the canal, this site was formerly a very extensive quarry, or, to use the local name, 'delph', which extended from just below Whitecote House, along to Newlay Canal Bridge.

Whitecote House. This early 19th-century house faces the canal near the bottom of Whitecote Lane.

7. NEWLAY CANAL BRIDGE

This is the first of the original stone-built canal bridges downstream from Rodley. Note the grooves at each side of the arch, where vertical wooden rollers prevented the tow-ropes of the horse-drawn barges from rubbing against the masonry. Further grooves cut into the stone kerb of the towpath, and into the masonry opposite, beneath the centre of the bridge, were for stop-planks, which could be slotted in to stop the flow of water during repairs etc. The bridge also bears a number of marks, the triangles and single vertical lines being used by quarrymen or masons to identify their individual blocks, while the arrow-head on the upstream side is an ordnance survey bench-mark, 183.5ft above sea level.

Here the trail divides, one section continuing on the towpath towards

Kirkstall and Leeds, (see no. 15 below) while the other turns off the towpath, and proceeds to Newlay Bridge, only a few minutes walk downhill.

8. THE ABBEY INN

Probably built in the mid-18th century, the Abbey Inn is a typical example of local vernacular architecture. Despite its rural location, it used to enjoy a good level of trade from travellers crossing Newlay Bridge, as well as the local quarrymen, forgemen and dyers. In 1899 it was owned by Whitaker Brothers of the adjacent dyeworks, apparently as a means of controlling the drinking habits of their workforce. Having passed through the hands of the Bradford Dyers Association and Richard Whitaker & Sons (Brewers), it was eventually bought by Whitbread & Co., then owners of Kirkstall Brewery.

The Abbey Inn at Newlay, which provided refreshments for the local quarrymen, forgemen and dyers.

21

9. St Margaret's Church

The field just opposite the inn, near the entrance to Hunter's Greave, the Airedale District Scout Activity Centre, is the site of St Margaret's Church, a corrugated iron building opened on 29th July 1891. Attached to the parish of Bramley, it not only served the religious needs of the local community, but also acted as a focus for its social life, having an active choir, orchestra, theatrical group and pierrots, as well as cricket and tennis groups, garden parties, at homes, picnics and excursions from Newlay Station. Unfortunately the church was destroyed by fire on 20th October 1908, and was replaced by a new church further up Pollard Lane, at the opposite side of the canal.

10. The Aire Vale Dyeworks

From 1859 this factory was successfully operated by the firm of Haigh and Billington, but a period of bad trade forced them to close down in 1877, when Whitaker Brothers purchased the works for £27,000. Although badly damaged by fire in August 1890, the dyeworks were soon back in operation, and gradually rebuilt, the office block with its arched windows being completed in 1907.

These works concentrated on Bradford and Manchester cloth, much of it being dyed black using aniline dyes which had been introduced here by Charles Carter, who had visited Germany to learn how to carry out the necessary processes. The finished products were then exported all over the world, large quantities going to India, South America, East and West Africa and Egypt.

11. Newlay Station

The Leeds and Bradford Railway opened on 30th May 1846, when a Directors' Train decorated with flowers and flags inscribed 'See the conquering hero come' and 'Who'd have thought it' ran through Newlay. Wooden platforms for the first station here were erected in September 1846, the Midland Railway, which took over the line in 1851, later making considerable improvements. A new station and a road bridge over the railway was completed in 1892, while in 1904-6 the number of tracks was increased from two to four.

The station provided a vital transport facility for the local industries, receiving some 27,000 tons of goods, minerals and coal, and dispatching some 10,000 tons of goods and minerals each year in the late 1950s. In addition it had a well-used parcel service, and over 32,000 passenger ticket sales, but even this level of activity could not protect it from the sweeping cuts of the 1960s. The goods services were withdrawn in September 1963, and passenger services in March 1965, after which the station was demolished.

12. High Mill

This mill stood on the downstream side of the road between Newlay Station and Newlay Bridge. Used for woollen manufacture by Messrs Musgrave & Co. in 1823, and later by Samuel Hird as a weaving shed, it had become an oil works by the early 20th century. Here A. Hess & Brother made fatty acids from tallow and palm oil, distilled grease from local woollen mills to obtain cloth oil, and also refined lubricating oils.

This has been the site of an important river crossing for centuries, one of the deeds of Kirkstall Abbey, which owned a grange here on the north bank of the river, describing it as 'the ford of Horsforth' in 1154-75. It is probable that the monks built the first bridge here, about 50 yards upstream, but this had become unusable by the early 17th century, when traffic had reverted to using the old ford. To remedy this situation, James Cootes of Headingley offered £80 towards the construction of a new bridge. As the total cost was estimated to be some £130, Sir John Savile, tenant of the Forge, requested additional financial support from other townships, pointing out that it was used by the inhabitants 'of the west part of this shire to travel towards York, being a direct waye from the most part of the forrest of Knaresburrow, the parishes of Otley, Leathley and Harwood to Adwalton fairs, for fetching of coals and other necessaris'. On 4th June 1656, William Quippe and William Myers, wallers, of Guiseley were commissioned to build the new bridge, the principal local inhabitants being instructed to provide 'sleds or carrs', draught animals and labourers, to carry stone to the site, and retrieve materials from the old bridge ready for re-use.

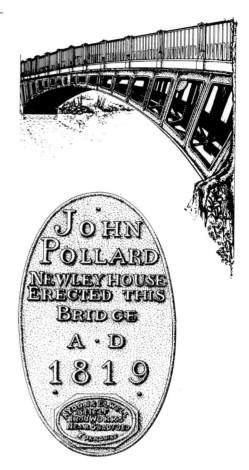

Built by John Pollard in 1819, Newlay Bridge is now one of the oldest cast-iron bridges in the county. After giving good service for some 170 years, its use is now restricted to foot passengers.

If this bridge was completed, it did not last for long, for by 1776 there was no recollection of a bridge here 'in the memory of the oldest man living' and a ford had become well-established 200 yards downstream. In 1783 John Pollard, a local landowner, built a new toll bridge here, replacing it by the present cast-iron bridge made by Aydon and Elwell of Shelf Iron Works in 1819, at the cost of £1,500. One of the oldest iron bridges in the county, it is composed of segmental arched cast-iron ribs inter-connected by cast-iron lattice braces stayed by wrought-iron rods. The tolls collected at the house on the downstream side of the bridge were very profitable, and to break this monopoly a Newlay Bridge Company, backed by the Horsforth Board and the Midland Railway, erected a free footbridge a short distance downstream in 1886. As a result of the ensuing litigation, the iron bridge was made toll-free in 1887 in return for a £500 payment in compensation. As the volume and weight of traffic increased, a two-ton 3 mph limit was imposed in 1930, the bridge being finally closed to traffic following an extensive restoration programme funded by the British Railways Board and the West Yorkshire Metropolitan County Council in 1984. After serving as an important river crossing for over 800 years, Newlay Bridge is now a very peaceful location, its transport role having been superseded by the Leeds Ring Road bridges at Rodley, a mile to the west.

14. KIRKSTALL FORGE WEIR

The weir just downstream from Newlay Bridge was first built around 1690 to provide additional water power for operating Kirkstall Forge. The supply was drawn off through a sluice at the north side of the weir, and conducted down a goit to a former dam adjacent to the forge building. It had to be regularly cleared by workmen from the forge, a task which could take two weeks to complete. In 1796 they received two shillings (10p) a day for this, plus free food and beer.

From this point Newlay Lane may be followed up to the main A65 road for buses back to Kirkstall and Leeds. Alternatively, walk back to Newlay Canal Bridge and rejoin the towpath.

15. THE SAND & GRAVEL CHUTE

The low stone building on the opposite bank was probably built as a warehouse and later used to load sand directly into barges for transport along the canal. During the early 20th century, up to around 1913, John Micklethwaite operated as a sand merchant here, being followed by the Newlay Sand & Gravel Company up to around 1930, and then A. & R. Briggs up to the 1950s.

16. NEWLAY LOCKS

These three-rise locks, built of the local stone, with the traditional oak gates, raise the canal 26ft 11in. Note the paddle gear, which controls the flow of water. These vary from lock to lock down the canal. From here the heavily-wooded Hawksworth valley can be seen extending northwards beyond the River Aire. In the early 13th century the monks diverted its stream, Cow Beck, along a goit to a dam above Kirkstall Abbey, so that they could flush their drains etc. into the river. In the 16th century this water supply was adapted to power Kirkstall Forge.

Here the trail divides, one route proceeding down the towpath towards Leeds, while the other crosses the footbridge over the middle lock, joins the track on the low embankment at the edge of the wood, and proceeds downstream, parallel to the canal. Both routes rejoin at Kirkstall Forge Locks (no. 18) half a mile away.

17. BRAMLEY FALL

The present woodland occupies the site of a very extensive series of quarries which produced much of the excellent gritstone used to construct the canal and many other buildings along the waterfront.

The opening of the Leeds and Liverpool Canal enabled commercial potential of the stone to be fully exploited. In June 1777, the local newspapers announced that the quarry in 'Bramley Upper Fall ... by the side of the Grand Canal' had been opened. Under a lease from the Earl of Cardigan, James Oddie built up a country-wide market for Bramley Fall stone, its resilience to water and to impact making it ideal for civil engineering and defensive works. He supplied it for building the Aire and Calder, Foss, and Market Weighton Navigations, Hull and Wapping docks, and the Martello towers which defended the Essex, Kent and Sussex coasts against Napoleon's intended invasion. In 1811, following Mr Oddie's death in the previous year, Messrs Spink, Rogerson and Waddington took over the lease, trading as Bramley Fall Quarries, and continued to expand the trade.

The larger blocks, weighing perhaps eight or ten tons, were levered from the quarry face, raised to the surface by cranes powered by horse-gins, and lowered on to strong solid-wheeled trucks for haulage to the dressing shops, where masons worked them to the required shape. Smaller blocks were carried by the 'big huggers', quarrymen of enormous strength, who wore heavy leather shoulder-guards to protect themselves from the roughness of their loads.

During the mid-19th century these quarries provided stone for many important building projects, including

the base of Leeds Town Hall, and a number of bridges and railway structures seen along the Waterways Heritage Trail. By the early 1900s, however, the supplies of good stone began to run out, the 69 acre Bramley Fall estate then being acquired by Leeds City Council in 1903 for use as a park and public woodland. A path branching up the hill through the former quarry workings now leads to a picnic area, gardens and a car park, while a further path descending by shallow steps towards the canal follows the trail down to Kirkstall Forge Locks.

This early 19th-century view of Bramley Fall shows the quarries in operation, with a huge block being loaded onto a barge for transport to some distant civil engineering project. The buildings of Kirkstall Forge appear in the woods to the left, and the tower of the Abbey in the distance.

This 18th-century helve-hammer shop still stands in the middle of the present Kirkstall Forge. The cast-iron water-wheel turned the cam on the right-hand side, which raised the enormous hammer and allowed it to drop four times per revolution.

18. KIRKSTALL FORGE LOCKS

Here the trail crosses the locks, which are a 'listed building', by means of footbridges. From the foot of the three-rise Forge Locks (23ft 6in rise) there is a good view of Kirkstall Forge.

19. KIRKSTALL FORGE

Having completed 400 years of continuous production, the forge is one of the most interesting of the trail's historic sites.

After the Dissolution of 1539, when there was no longer any need for the goit which carried water from Hawksworth Woods to the dam above Kirkstall Abbey,

John, Lord Savile, the new landowner, realised that it had good potential for industrial use and established a bloomery to transform iron-ore into wrought-iron here, probably a little before 1600. On 10th May 1618, he leased the forge, with all its buildings, watercourses, flood-gates, streams, Hawksworth Woods, etc. to Sir Francis Fane, Sir Edward Barrett, Robert Leigh and George Hemsworth. Under this partnership, the forge was improved by the construction of a finery forge which made wrought-iron from blast-furnace iron around 1640. In 1658 the forge was leased to three London merchants, Bancks, Allsop and Fownes, who transferred it to Thomas Dickin and

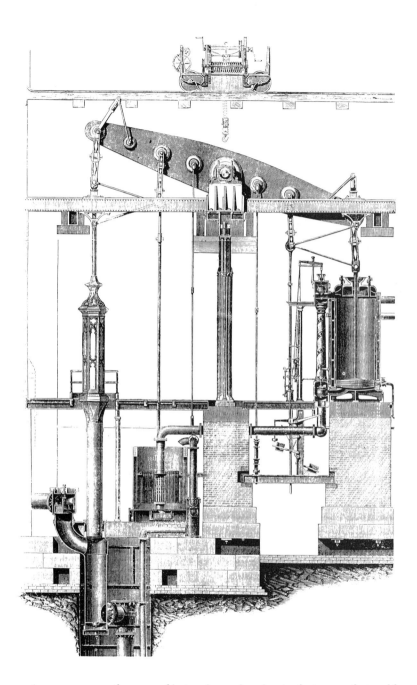

Beam engines were among the range of impressive engineering products manufactured by Kirkstall Forge in the mid-19th century. This example, with its splendid Gothic details, was made for Croydon Waterworks around 1868.

William Cotton in 1676, who immediately sold a third share to John Spencer of Cannon Hall, Barnsley. When a new lease was granted to Thomas Dickin in 1690, the rent was increased from £80 to £131 a year, reflecting the growing size of the forge, especially since a new weir and goit had now been constructed at Newlay to power a slitting mill to roll and slit the iron into narrow strips. From this time through to 1757, Kirkstall Forge formed part of the Spencer's group of ironworks, processing English, Dutch, Polish, Swedish and even American iron into a variety of rods, bars etc. John and Richard Crookes then took over the forge up to 1778-9, when it passed into the control of the Beecroft and Butler families, who were to operate it for the next 200 years.

During the late 18th century the forge was enlarged by building new slitting mills, workshops, cottages, a chapel, a grocery and a brew-house, to make it an almost self-contained community. Raw materials brought in by canal were now being manufactured into finished goods, such as spades, shovels, screws, patten-rings, fenders, fire-irons, coal boxes, gridirons, frying pans, pudding dishes, smith's vices and hammers, axes, files, scythes etc. Many of these products were exported to America, Canada, Russia and other parts of the world. The late 1830s and early 1840s saw the introduction of steam-engines to power the forge, and the establishment of engineering workshops, where horizontal steam-engines, pumping sets, cranes, turntables, swing bridges, drop-hammers and presses, often of very large size, were now constructed. A period of bad trade, however, forced the forge to reconsider its range of products, and to close its engineering workshops in 1878. Now it concentrated on the manufacture of best Yorkshire iron railway lines and axles, vehicle axles, forgings, anvils, bar iron and rolled shafting, for which new drop stamps, drawbenches and rolling mills were installed. Over the following years axles for road vehicles became the forge's major product, the 1920s seeing complete braked-axle units being made in large numbers.

In 1974, the 200-year connection with the Butler family was broken, when the forge was acquired by GKN Axles. Between 1977 and 1982 they completed a £12 million investment programme to provide a streamlined assembly process for axles for trucks, buses, military and off-highway vehicles, cranes, fork-lifts etc., raising production capacity up to 50,000 axles each year which still continues today. There is no public access to the site, but, behind the modern buildings, the 18th-century water-powered helve hammer shop, complete with its water-wheels and hammers, still survives intact.

From here, follow the towpath downstream towards Kirkstall.

20. KIRKSTALL LOCK

This single-rise lock raises the canal 5ft 7in. There are good views of Kirkstall Abbey from here, while in the distance rises the tower of St Stephen's Church, Kirkstall. This church was built in 1828-9 to the designs of the Leeds architect, R.D. Chantrell. Richard Oastler, the

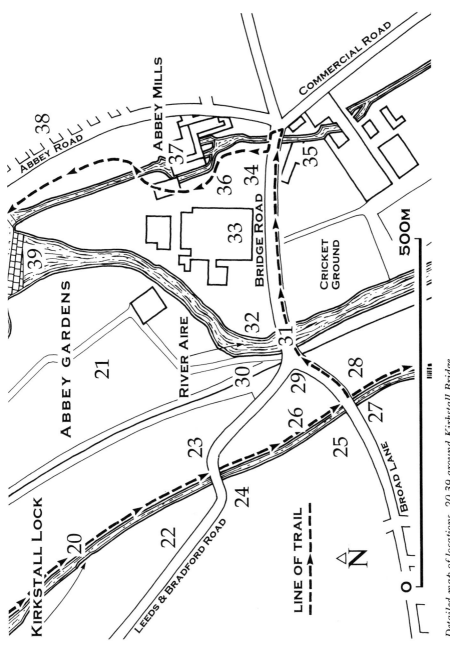

Detailed map of locations 20-39 around Kirkstall Bridge

KIRKSTALL LOCK

ABBEY GARDENS

RIVER AIRE

LEEDS & BRADFORD ROAD

BROAD LANE

BRIDGE ROAD

CRICKET GROUND

ABBEY MILLS

ABBEY ROAD

COMMERCIAL ROAD

LINE OF TRAIL

N

0 1 500M

20
21
22
23
24
25
26
27
28
29
30
31
32
33
34
35
36
37
38
39

'Factory King' largely responsible for the Ten Hours Bill, which greatly improved the conditions of men, women and children in factories, was buried here in 1861, being commemorated in one of its stained glass windows.

21. THE RHUBARB FIELDS

The fields stretching from Kirkstall Lock towards the Abbey were used for growing rhubarb. It was a Yorkshireman, Sir Matthew Lister, who first introduced garden rhubarb (*Rheum rhaponticum*) into England from Italy around 1620. At first it was appreciated for the medicinal qualities of its root, but then, from the 1780s, the chopped stalks began to be used as a substitute for gooseberries in pies. The real development of the local rhubarb or 'tusky' industry took place in these fields in the late 1870s when Joseph Whitwell erected forcing sheds here. After two years in the fields, the roots were ploughed up and arranged in beds in the perfect darkness of these sheds, where coal or coke furnaces maintained them at 55°F. After four to six weeks, with regular watering, the buds burst with an audible popping sound, the richly pink stalks and tiny yellow leaves then growing rapidly until they were picked by hand, the pickers using only a candle for illumination, since any brighter light would spoil both the quality and the colour.

The first supplies could be ready by early December, one writer noting in 1904 that 'Leeds is famous, it might be said throughout Europe, for its early rhubarb, and already the first pale sticks of this luscious comestible have been seen in the city, while even agents from Paris are also on the scene'. By this time the despatch of rhubarb to London by rail was already a well-established practice, the Great Northern's 'Rhubarb Train' leaving Leeds with between 60 and 160 tons of rhubarb every evening so as to be in time for the early morning fruit market at Covent Garden.

22. THE ELLARS

The house on the opposite side of the canal takes its name from the former fields here, where elm-trees once grew. The present late Georgian house, with its flanking Victorian wings, was the home of William Tattersall, who operated a large maltings here from the 1840s to the 1860s.

23. THE LEEDS AND BRADFORD ROAD BRIDGE

During the late 18th and early 19th centuries the volume of traffic along the Leeds and Bradford Road increased

Turner's view of 1824 shows, from left to right, quarrymen in Monk Wood, The Ellars, Kirkstall Lock, and Kirkstall Abbey. This great artist visited Kirkstall on a number of occasions, filling his sketchbooks with rapid impressions of the Abbey and its surrounding countryside.

considerably, making it necessary to carry out major improvements. The old route from Kirkstall Bridge took a direct line up the steepest side of the valley, putting considerable strain on the horses. To remedy this, a new road was constructed sometime between 1811 and 1822 to take a much easier gradient along the side of the valley, passing over this new bridge and continuing above Bramley Fall to Stanningley.

24. MONK WOOD

The wooded area at the opposite side of the canal conceals a number of powerful springs of crystal-clear water. In 1715, Ralph Thoresby described this 'noted well ... near which Lead Pipes have been found in the Ground, whence it's supposed that this spring-water was conveyed beyond the River for the Use of the Abbey, which is directly opposite it'. In 1863 the four major springs were diverted into a series of collection tanks and a 14ft by 40ft reservoir, to supply water directly into the adjacent brewery.

Around 1824 J.M.W. Turner, the great English watercolourist, sat at the top of Monk Wood to paint his view of 'Kirkstall Lock on the River Aire', which was later engraved to illustrate W.B. Cooke's *Rivers of England* of 1827. The original has a wonderful luminous quality, and shows a wealth of detail, including quarrymen working at the water's edge, sailing barges, and a coach going across the Leeds and Bradford Road bridge.

25. KIRKSTALL BREWERY

In 1793 Sir James Graham divided Monk Wood into plots, leasing one to Henry Cooper, and the other, nearest to Leeds, to Joseph Musgrave, for 300 years. Henry Cooper immediately began to develop this new property, erecting a huge maltings and a wharf on the canal side, and well built houses, Cooper House and Poplar House, for himself and his maltster.

Joseph Musgrave erected similar maltings, cottages and a house, Grove House, on his plot, these being operated by Ephraim Elsworth from 1814 to 1832, after which they passed to Joseph's eldest son, Simeon. In 1833 Thomas Walker of Hunslet purchased the maltings for £7,000, and converted them into a very well-equipped brewery, but the expense proved far too much for him. By 1844 he had died bankrupt, and the brewery reverted to Simeon Musgrave, who was still owed the original purchase money. Simeon now sold the brewery to Benjamin Dawson & Co., who expanded both the trade and the buildings between 1847 and 1869, the huge four-storey block on the right being built in 1867 on the site of Henry Cooper's old maltings. After Benjamin Dawson's death in 1869, the ownership of the company fell into dispute, this being resolved by a sale in 1872, when it was purchased by the Kirkstall Brewery Company for £22,400.

About this time, the brewery was producing 26,000 barrels of beer each year, but, by re-equipping the plant, and building a high tower brewery, annual production had almost tripled to 72,000 barrels by 1898. These vast supplies of India Pale Ales, strong ale, mild ale, light bitter, imperial stout, double stout and

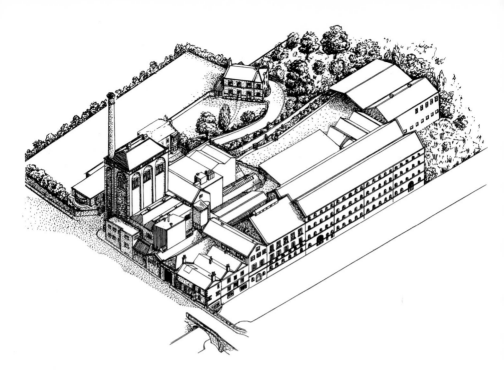

Kirkstall Brewery started in the former maltings close to Broad Lane canal bridge in 1833, expanding over the next 150 years to the 115,000 sq. ft plant seen here. Notable features include the late 19th-century tower brewery to the left, Henry Cooper's house of around 1793 at the top, and the massive racking block of 1867 on the right. Through its arched doorways barrels of beer were loaded into barges for export to Australia and New Zealand.

porter were not only sold in Leeds and Yorkshire, but were carried to much more distant locations. A London depot was established, and this was followed by an enormous trans-Atlantic trade. Great hogsheads of beer were run out of the arches at water level on to Aire and Calder Navigation Company boats which carried them downstream to Goole, where they were transhipped onto the company's own steamships, the 953 ton ss *Charante*, and the 1,831 ton ss *Kirkstall* of 1895, the latter having high-pressure boilers made by Samson Fox at the Leeds Forge. From Goole, these ships commenced the longest beer run in the world, delivering their cargoes to Australia and New Zealand before returning for fresh supplies.

In 1936, the brewery was taken over by Dutton's of Blackburn, producing their Green Label, No. 3 and Pale Ale for sale in the Blackburn area, their waggons bringing back Dutton's Old Ben Draught, 'OBJ' (Oh be Joyful) and Mercer's Meat Stout up to the 1939-45 World War, when this trade had to cease due to zoning restrictions. After going into liquidation in 1954, the brewery was sold to Whitbread's of London, who completely re-equipped its plant, enabling it to produce over 62,000 barrels of Mackeson stout each year by

1957. Further additions brought the production of bitter and best mild up to 250,000 barrels, but then changing economic circumstances and changing tastes brought a reduction in demand, with the result that Whitbread's closed the brewery in January 1983, thus ending a 150-year tradition of brewing fine beers and stout in the Kirkstall valley.

26. THE MALTINGS

The stone buildings on the towpath side of the canal, just opposite the brewery, formed part of a 150ft long maltings built by Simeon Musgrave around 1829. They were sold to Thomas Walker in 1833, after which they continued to produce the malt required for the brewery up to the time of their demolition around 1960.

27. BROAD LANE CANAL BRIDGE

This is one of the original canal bridges, constructed to carry the early roadway from Kirkstall up Broad lane, or Bramley Hill, to the hilltop weaving village of Bramley. From the 1740s at least, this formed part of a major cross-country transport route, linking the important textile towns of Halifax and Bradford with Leeds, and the inland port of Selby, some 20 miles downstream. Note the arrow, cross, line and 'W' masons' marks on this bridge.

28. KING'S WHARF

During the early 1900s, this wharf was operated by J.W. King, agent to the Leeds and Liverpool Canal Company. Here barges delivered both coal, for the local industries and private houses, and imported barley, for the nearby maltings. Here is a public car park and seating.

Here the trail divides, one section continuing on the towpath towards Leeds (see no. 44) while the other turns northwards to Kirkstall Abbey and Abbey House. The route to the Abbey proceeds away from the towpath, across Wyther Lane, and along the south side of Bridge Road to the junction with Abbey Road, and Commercial Road.

29. HOLLYBUSH FARM

The earliest building on this site is the barn, which probably dates from the late 17th century. Originally its roof was supported by two rows of great oak posts, leaving narrow aisles down each side of the interior. This was replaced by a new single-span roof early in the 19th century, when the adjoining farmhouse was also rebuilt. The farm now forms a base for the British Trust for Conservation Volunteers (B.T.C.V.) a registered charity which promotes practical environmental work

Hollybush Farm is now the Leeds base of the British Trust for Conservation Volunteers, which undertakes numerous conservation works throughout the district, including sections of the Waterfront Trail.

throughout Britain. The trust has established a plant nursery here, and continues to carry out a wide variety of environmental improvements within this section of the Aire valley. Here is a picnic area with tables, benches etc.

30. KIRKSTALL STATION

This section of the Leeds and Bradford Railway was opened on 31st April 1846, a fine stone built station being erected at the northern side of the bridge. In 1903, the present iron bridge was widened to 50 ft to accommodate the increased road traffic. Regrettably the station was closed in 1965, and subsequently demolished, thus removing a valuable transport facility from the people of Kirkstall, as well as making it much more difficult for visitors from along the Morecambe and Settle-Carlisle lines to visit Kirkstall Abbey.

31. KIRKSTALL BRIDGE

Probably the first bridge on this site was built by monks of Kirkstall Abbey during the medieval period. This bridge had become unusable by 1616, when plans were drawn up for a new single-arched bridge. It was a large undertaking, with 340 piles driven into the river bed, 17,000 arch stones, extensive works at both ends of the bridge, 'battlements' of stone, etc., but it was completed by June, 1619, when the builder, John Philip, was paid £132 16s 8d for its construction. It did not last for long, however. On the morning of 23rd January 1643, Sir Thomas Fairfax and his Parliamentary army of six troops of horse, three troops of dragoons, 2,000 clubmen and 1,000 musketeers marched down the valley from Bradford to Kirkstall Bridge where he intended to divide his forces into two, one group to go south, and the other north, to encircle Royalist Leeds. Here they found that the defenders had

This photograph of 1912 shows the newly-completed Kirkstall bridge, designed by W.T. Lancashire, the City Engineer. The City's coat of arms is carved just above the cut-waters of its stone piers.

broken the bridge, so that he had to march upstream to Apperley Bridge, in order to get his troops across to the north bank, and on to Woodhouse Moor.

After the Civil War, the bridge was rebuilt, a programme of widening and repair in 1778-9 producing a 22ft wide roadway carried on three 45ft arches. Unfortunately it was still too narrow and by 1906 was failing to meet the heavy demands being made upon it, arch stones were collapsing, and a three-ton limit was imposed. To remedy this situation, W.T. Lancashire, the City Engineer, designed the present bridge, which was constructed with stone piers bearing the City arms, and ironwork by John Butler & Co. of Stanningley decorated with Romanesque details to reflect the architecture of the Abbey. It was opened by Alderman Lupton, Chairman of the Improvement Committee, on 28th June 1912.

32. THE BRIDGE INN

This inn first opened in the early 19th century as the Horse and Jockey, changing to its present name around 1840. For many years it was a tied house of Kirkstall Brewery, but it is now a free house, with attractive bars and a riverside beer-garden at the rear.

33. THRIFT STORES CENTRAL WAREHOUSE

Thrift Stores first started with a single grocer's shop in Holbeck in south Leeds in 1881. From this time the company expanded rapidly, developing a very extensive chain of stores. The large premises now occupied by the Clover Home Furnishing Centre was built as Thrift's central warehouse and bakery in 1929-32, up to 2,000 tons of groceries being dispatched from here to the branches every week. There is now a good coffee shop here.

34. KIRKSTALL WAR MEMORIAL

The tall Portland stone cross was erected, in its surrounding garden, to commemorate the 155 men from this village who lost their lives during the First World War. Their names are recorded on the cast-bronze panels at the back of the memorial.

35. THE STAR AND GARTER

The large stone building with two sets of Georgian bow windows, close to the cross-roads, is the former Star and Garter inn. Conveniently situated at the junction of the Leeds-Bradford and Leeds-Kendal roads, it was popular with coach travellers. One of its guests was Mrs Sarah Siddons, the great late 18th-century actress. Here, she wrote to Lady Harcourt, 'I set myself down for the advantage of pure air and perfect quiet, rather than lodge in Leeds, most disagreeable town in His Majesty's dominions, God bless him. I have played these four nights, and am very tired of Kirkstall Abbey. It is too sombre for a person of my age, and I am no antiquarien. It is, however, extremely beautiful.'

Cross Bridge Road, at the crossing here, and walk back along the opposite pavement to enter the gateway with the iron railings. This leads towards Kirkstall Abbey.

36. KIRKSTALL LIGHT RAILWAY

Constructed in the early 1980s, this railway carries visitors to and from the Abbey grounds, on some weekends and holiday periods during the summer months, often using Leeds-built narrow-gauge locomotives.

37. ABBEY MILLS

The mill race here, locally called a 'goit', was probably cut in the 12th century by the monks of Kirkstall Abbey to provide power for one of their corn mills. After the Dissolution, the monks' small steep-gabled stone-built corn mill appears to have continued in use through to the late 18th century. In his diary for 3rd November 1799, Thomas Butler of Kirkstall Forge noted that the mills 'were all in one Flame, and on my arrival there I did not think that one stone could be saved, but shortly after 2 or 3 Engines came from Leeds, attended by our Mayor, our worthy Captain Benjamin Gott. By his exertions and encouragement the men were very much spirited, and they played the engines with such force that about 2 oc. the Fire was got under and the Oil Mills saved. Capt. Gott exerted himself wonderfully & I do think rather imprudently - yet I do believe all that is standing of the building is owing to him ... the damage

In September 1807, a visitor to the Star & Garter sketched this view from the front of the inn. To the left, a turnstile leads to the serpentine walk up to the Abbey, while at the centre stand the Abbey Mills, powered by water in the goit, which flows downstream beneath the bridge on the right.

will be considerable, perhaps 6 or 7 thousand pounds'.

The mills were later rebuilt, and operated for corn and oil milling by Ephraim Elsworth in the 1820s, then by Brady and Rowntree up to around 1850. From the 1820s other parts of the mills were used for the manufacture of woollen cloth, Obediah Willans working here from around 1826 to the mid-1830s, followed by Ephraim Elsworth, worsted spinner, Abraham Webster & Sons, woollen manufacturers from 1847 to 1886, and finally John Bradley & Sons, woollen manufacturers, from whom the City Council purchased the mills in 1961. Today the mills are used to house a variety of light industries.

The main features to be seen today include the pre-1711 bypass channel running between the footpath and the mills, and the extensive masonry platform built sometime between 1822 and 1834, beneath which pass the mill races. The mill building (now demolished to window sill level) directly across the bypass channel probably dated from this period too, the three-storey block behind being constructed earlier in the 19th century, utilising burnt gritstone blocks recovered from its burnt-out predecessor.

An interesting local scene was observed here by a visitor walking up to the Abbey in 1865. He passed this 'large stone factory or woollen mill, whence from within issued the thuds and groans and clatter of an agonised machinery. Under and around this modern mill, the water flowed with an inky blackness. In the field closely adjoining the consecrated precincts a number of stout buxom lasses were spreading long and heavy fabrics on the ground to bleach, laughing and playing all sorts of pranks with some companions of the baser sex!'

The path continues on, past the mills, and over the footbridge to enter the grounds of Kirkstall Abbey.

38. THE VESPERS, NORMANS, AND DE LACYS

The block of terrace houses seen on the opposite side of Kirkstall Road are typical of thousands which were built in Leeds from the mid-19th century. They take their names from Vespers, the monks' evening prayers, and the Norman family of De Lacy, who founded the abbey. The first terraces, the Vespers, and Norman Street, Row, Grove and Mount, were built as back-to-backs in 1903-6, De Lacy Mount of 1906-10 being through houses. Norman Mount, View and Row were completed in 1932-7 as some of the last back-to-backs in this country. Even though the erection of this type of house had been prohibited in 1909, schemes for which permission had been granted were still allowed to proceed.

39. THE WEIR

The present weir appears to have been constructed in the late 18th century, but it probably replaced one built by the monks in the mid-12th century, especially since it lies precisely at the end of the wall which enclosed their 40-acre precinct. In addition to holding fish stocks, it would also have permitted rafts of stone to be floated down from

37

quarries upstream, and to have provided power for a water mill. In 1804, there was only a simple wooden sluice-gate here, the present stone-built sluices and the adjoining Gothic lodge being constructed some time before 1834.

40. KIRKSTALL ABBEY

Kirkstall Abbey is Britain's finest early monastic ruin. Completed between 1152 and 1182, it still stands substantially complete up to its full height, its massive structure presenting a unique example of early Cistercian architecture.

In 1147 a community of Cistercian monks led by the dynamic Abbot Alexander left Fountains Abbey near Ripon to found a monastery on the lands of Henry de Lacy in the Pennine village of Barnoldswick. Here the local people and the climate combined to make life so difficult that a new site had to be found. While passing down the Aire valley on his way to Pontefract Castle, Alexander came upon a pleasant stretch of country well stocked with timber, stone and water, and inhabited by a group of hermits.

As this land was held by William of Poitou, a vassal of Henry de Lacy, the Abbot was able to use Henry's influence to gain possession of the site. On 19th May 1152, the monks moved from Barnoldswick to Kirkstall, to build here their great monastery dedicated to the Virgin Mary.

At first all the buildings were of wood, but almost immediately these began to be replaced by Bramley Fall gritstone, quarried nearby. The coarse texture and

hard-wearing qualities of this stone were ideal for producing the very strong, simple forms so characteristic of late Norman Cistercian architecture, in which decoration was reduced to the absolute minimum. So quickly did the work proceed, that the church, the cloister, and all its surrounding buildings were completed within the lifetime of Abbot Alexander, who died in 1182.

Over the next four centuries Kirkstall Abbey fulfilled its prime purpose in the worship of God. Wearing their white woollen habits or robes beneath a black scapular or cowl, the Choir Monks

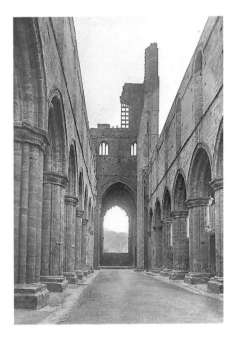

The nave of the Abbey church is a magnificent example of early transitional architecture. Before the great east window was inserted, a unique wheel window with interlacing tracery occupied the wall above the high altar.

Kirkstall Abbey is the most complete early monastic ruin in Britain, most of its massive stone buildings of 1152-82 still standing to full height. This view shows the great central tower added by Abbot William Marshall in the early 16th century.

39

maintained an almost continuous series of services from matins at around 2 am to compline at 7 pm every day. They occupied the eastern side of the Abbey, close to the high altar and chapels which would be entered directly from their dormitory.

Being literate, they used the cloister, the book cupboard and the library for study and writing, while the chapter house and the refectory provided accommodation for their meetings and their meals respectively.

The western side of the Abbey was occupied by the brown-robed Lay Brothers. Although they took the same vows as the Choir Monks, they were unable to read, and spent most of the time in practical labour. The economic prosperity of the whole community depended on their efficient management of the Abbey's granges and farms, and on their craft skills. The Lay Brothers held their services in the western end of the church, while their separate dormitory, refectory and stores etc. were in the adjoining west range. The life-style of all the monks was both simple and austere; a strict rule of silence was generally observed, the diet, at least in the early years, excluded all meat, and there was no heating except in the kitchens and warming house. It is recorded that for this reason the Kirkstall monks packed their stockings with hay to keep their feet warm in the cold winter months.

Over the following centuries further infirmaries, Abbot's lodgings, guest houses, etc., were constructed, but Kirkstall never had sufficient funds to undertake major rebuilding. In the early 16th century, however, the appearance of the Abbey was considerably changed by Abbot William Marshall, who renewed the roofs of the church, adding battlements, corner turrets, and a great central tower bearing his initials. Times were changing, however, and on 22nd November 1539, monastic life at Kirkstall came to an abrupt end when Abbot John Ripley surrendered the Abbey to Henry VIII's commissioners. After the Dissolution, the Abbey passed first to Thomas Cranmer, Archbishop of Canterbury, reverting to the Crown following his execution in 1556. In 1583-4 it was purchased by Sir Robert Savile, his family retaining it until 1671, when it passed by marriage into the hands of the Brudenells, Earls of Cardigan. Once stripped of its roofs, windows and furnishings, the building became overgrown with trees and bushes, soon acquiring the aspect of picturesque ruin, this being enhanced by the rustic milk-maids and cows which now occupied the site. Romantic poets and writers such as Walpole, Gray and Southey, and artists including Girtin, Cotman and Turner, all came here to bask amid 'The gloom of these ancient cells, the shade and verdure of the landscape, the glittering and murmer of the stream, the lofty towers, and long perspective of the Church'. Thus it remained until the sale of the Cardigan Estates in 1889.

In that year, the Abbey was purchased by Colonel John North, a local man who had made millions in the South American nitrate, silver, gas and railway industries. He immediately presented it to the City of Leeds for the enjoyment of its people. Having taken the best advice available, the City then commenced an extensive and very necessary conservation programme, stripping away all the roots which were literally tearing the buildings apart, removing tons of rubble, re-pointing the masonry, and setting out the grounds. Once this had been completed, the Abbey was opened to the public by the Lord Bishop of Ripon and the Lord Mayor of Leeds on 14th September 1895.

Since 1979, the City Council have commenced a major programme of conservation works on the Abbey ruins, appointing the first permanent team of masons, and erecting the first roof over the presbytery, since the early 16th century.

Walk round to the west front of the Abbey Church, from where the following route points to most of its significant features.

a. The Stables

Here visitors to the Abbey would stable their horses.

b. The Guest House

This building, constructed during the 13th-15th centuries, took the form of a medieval manor house, its central great hall having a chamber or solar block to the north, and butteries, sculleries, bakehouse and kitchens to the south. It would be used by all the Abbey's most important guests.

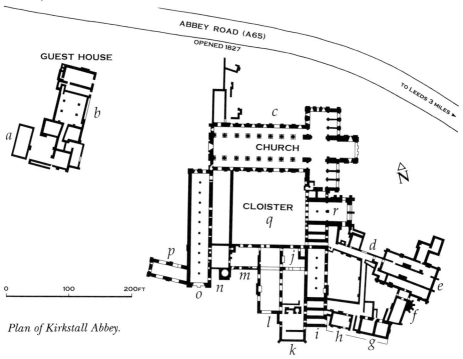

Plan of Kirkstall Abbey.

41

c. The Church

Virtually the whole church, up to the roof-line, was completed in the 1160s. Originally its interior was divided up into a number of separate spaces; from the west door, the length of the first four arches served as the Lay Brothers' nave, the fifth bay housed a pair of chapels, while the sixth was a retro-choir for aged and infirm monks. Here a great screen cut across the church, with a gallery above. The next two bays, and the area beneath the tower, formed the monks' choir from which they worshipped at the high altar in the presbytery at the east end. Extending to the sides of the choir, each transept provided three chapels for prayers and mass. The upper tower, battlements and corner turrets were added by Abbot William Marshall early in the 16th century.

d. The Infirmary Passages

Built as corridors in the 13th century, these passages were then given timber-framed first floors, probably providing a library and a long gallery for the Abbot's lodging.

e. The Infirmary

Built in the late 13th-14th centuries, this large central hall flanked by side-aisles housed the elderly monks and those who were sick or had just undergone bloodletting.

f. Visiting Abbot's Lodging

The Abbot of Fountains or his deputy would live here during the annual visitation, when they inspected the spiritual and general well-being of the Abbey. The foundations of a 15th-century bay window butt against the original 13th-century east wall.

g. The Infirmary Chapel

Erected in the early 13th century, this building housed the infirmary chapel on the first floor, a kitchen which served firstly the infirmary, and then the Abbot's lodging, being on the floor below.

h. The Abbot's Lodging

Here the Abbot lived in great comfort, his lodgings of c. 1230 having a basement for servants, a first floor main hall or guest-room, and a second floor solar or private living room. Both upper rooms had fireplaces, window-seats and screens passages.

i. Choir Monks' Reredorter

This block provided latrines for the Choir Monks' dormitory and the Abbot's lodgings. The grooves in the wall probably represent timber floors, seats and partitions.

j. The Warming House

Here a fire was lit for the monks between 1st November and Easter. The heat helped to keep the records dry in the muniment room above.

k. The Meat Kitchen

In the 15th century, it became customary to eat meat three times a week, provided that it was cooked in a separate kitchen and eaten in a separate room. For this reason, this new meat kitchen, with its great roasting hearths and ovens, was built next to the refectory. A dove-cote and fishponds used to stand just to the south of this room.

l. The Refectory

Built as a single large room in the late 12th century, this room was divided in the 15th century to provide a *misericord* where meat was eaten on the ground floor, and a refectory above for the normal vegetarian diet.

m. The Kitchen

Here, around a large fireplace, the food was cooked for the monks. The Choir Monks' food was passed through a serving hatch into their refectory, while that for the Lay Brothers went through a separate hatch into the Lay Brothers' refectory in the west range.

n. The Lane

These wide 12th-century arches gave access to the Lay Brothers' lane, which was separated from the cloister by a high stone wall. In the 15th century the archway was converted into a malthouse and bakehouse by adding the existing ovens and vat.

o. The West Range

The upper floor of this building was used as the Lay Brothers' dormitory, entered by a staircase against its east wall. The vaulted ground floor served as their refectory and cellarium or storehouse, and at the north end was an outer parlour where monks could meet

with outsiders. The western and southern walls collapsed around 1750.

p. The Lay-Brothers' Reredorter

This was the 12th-century Lay Brothers' latrine. A door leading from their dormitory gave access to a long row of cubicles arranged over the main drain.

q. The Cloister

This square 12th-century courtyard was surrounded by four arcades which gave covered access to all the major rooms. The west arcade, backing on to the Lay Brothers' lane, was used as a corridor, while that to the north probably served as a scriptorium where books were copied. The openings in the east arcade were (from the church southwards); the book cupboard, the library, the chapter house, the parlour (for conversations), the day stairs to the monks' dormitory, and the infirmary passage. Continuing along the south arcade are the door to the warming house, the towel cupboard, the lavatorium where the monks washed before dining, and the doors leading to the refectory, kitchens and malthouse.

r. The Chapter House

Here the community met with the Abbot each day to hear a chapter of the Rule of St Benedict, to confess faults, and transact its business. The 12th-century vestibule has its vaulted roof supported on stout clustered columns, while the roof of the Chapter House beyond consists of a single rib-vaulted span.

From the west of the Abbey, walk up the path to:

41. THE KIRKSTALL, ILKLEY AND SHIPLEY TURNPIKE

As with many early roads in West Yorkshire, the medieval route up the Aire valley ran on an elevated edge, conveniently above the wet riverside fields. The medieval road ran from Leeds, along Park Lane, Burley Road, Kirkstall Hill, Morris Lane and Spen Lane, the closure of the Abbey enabling a new route to be opened from Abbey Mills, directly through the Abbey church, and on to the forge and Newlay bridge.

By Act of Parliament dated 10th June 1825, this new turnpike road was constructed from Leeds, running north of the river to Kirkstall, where it proceeded through the Abbey precinct, and on towards Guiseley and Ilkley. It was opened in 1827. Across the road stands;

1830

This sketch shows Abbey House in 1830, ten years before it was converted from a farmhouse into an ironmaster's residence. The original gateway has been filled with a Gothic window, while to the left the medieval toilet or garderobe may be seen, together with the chimney of the porter's lodge.

By the 1890s, the Beecroft, Butler and Harding families had transformed Abbey House into a very comfortable Gothic-revival mansion, their additions, in Bramley Fall stone, blending admirably with the early monastic buildings at its core. Since 1927 it has been the City's folk museum.

42. ABBEY HOUSE MUSEUM

At the heart of Abbey House lies the great gatehouse of Kirkstall Abbey, which controlled access into the six-acre inner precinct. Built between 1152 and 1182, it still retains its original vaulted ceiling and a spiral staircase leading to a 13th century chapel above. After the Dissolution on 22nd November 1539, John Ripley, the last abbot, blocked up each end of the archway to make himself a house here, and was later buried under the floor, where he was found in the early 19th century.

After serving as a farmhouse for 300 years, Abbey House was restored and extended in 1841 to form the family home of George Skirrow Beecroft MP, of Kirkstall Forge. After his death in 1869 the house was extended even further by John Octavius Butler, another partner of Kirkstall Forge, after which it was leased from 1883 to 1889 to another ironmaster, Leonard Cooper of the Aireside Hematite Company. In 1893 it

44

Stephen Harding Gate, one of the reconstructions of 1890s Leeds streets which form a major feature of the Abbey House Museum.

was purchased by Col. T.W. Harding of T.R. Harding & Son's Tower Works, who fully restored it in medieval/Jacobean style, adding the ornamental ceilings, fine carved oak and stained glass which give it so much of its present character. After returning to the Butler family's occupation between 1912 and 1925, Abbey House was sold to Leeds City Council, who opened it as a folk museum in 1927. Today the house continues to be a major attraction in its own right, both as a fine Norman building, and as a 19th-century ironmaster's residence.

Between 1954 and 1958 the museum built three streets of 1890s period shops in the courtyards behind Abbey House. These feature eleven shops, six craft workshops, a cottage and a public house, all fully equipped with authentic furniture, fittings and contents, mainly from the Leeds area. In addition, there

are display galleries showing a selection of exhibits drawn from the museum's extensive high-quality collections of toys and games, costume and textiles, and fireplaces. The museum is much bigger than it looks from the outside, and visitors should allow between one and two hours to enjoy its varied contents.

43. DAMSTEADS AND VESPER GATE

On leaving Abbey House, cross Abbey Walk and enter the car park. The road called Vesper Lane, which runs across the field away from Abbey House, forms the top of a dam erected around 1200 to hold water collected by a goit from Hawksworth Woods, the next side-valley upstream. Stone-lined channels carried it from this dam, down through the Abbey, flushing the contents of the drains through into the river. Having survived intact for over 750 years, it was regrettably filled in, in the 1970s, to

45

make the car park and playing fields. The stone pillar at the far end of Vesper Lane is all that remains of the Vesper Gate, the western entrance into the Abbey precinct.

From this point, return to the main trail by retracing the route to King's Wharf, no. 28/44. Alternatively, buses from the stop on the main road, in front of Abbey House, go into Leeds city centre.

44. KING'S WHARF

Follow the towpath downstream, past some light industrial buildings and the site of the former brickworks across the canal, to the Wyther Canal Bridge at Amen Corner, which has a bench mark for 136- 7ft above sea level.

Here the trail divides, one route proceeding straight along the towpath to Redcote Bridge (no. 47), while the other goes over the bridge, turns left up Wyther Lane, past Warrens public house and a row of shops, and then branches left, up Armley Ridge Road, by the stone pillar which formed part of the estate wall for Gott's Park. This section of road was built largely at the expense of the Gott family in 1847 to create work for the unemployed.

45. GOTT'S PARK

The 73 acres of parkland to the north of Armley Ridge Road were purchased by Benjamin Gott, the leading woollen manufacturer of Georgian Yorkshire, in 1803. At first these grounds, which surround Armley House, were laid out by a Mr White, but in 1810 Humphrey Repton, the leading landscape architect of the day, was called in to re-model the whole park. Before his improvements, this hill-top was so bare and bleak that 'the wind from the moors, along the vale of Kirkstall, would rush through the small vestibule (of Armley House) with such violence as to render it hardly habitable'. To remedy this, and to provide a suitable setting for the house, Repton planted thick woods along the top of the ridge. These, together with new drives, gave 'the view of an interior lawn surrounded by wood, the more extended views shown under the branches of trees, which form an appropriate foreground to the distant scenery, increase the imaginary extent of the places by showing it particularly, and display its scenery by degrees, and in succession'.

In 1928 the Trustees of Wade's Charity, a major Leeds benefaction dating from 1530, purchased the park and presented it to the City of Leeds for public use. It now serves as one of the city's golf courses.

At the top of the hill, opposite the Ridge Cottages, where formerly, hand loom weavers worked, turn in between the stone gateposts, and walk towards Armley House. The walled garden nearby was formerly used to produce vegetables and fruit for the house, but is now an attractive rose garden.

46. ARMLEY HOUSE

In 1718 Thomas Woolrich, a local merchant, built a relatively plain house on this site. Since it lacked both the scale and quality required by its new owner, Benjamin Gott, it was completely re-cased and extended in fine ashlar between 1810 and 1822.

The architect was Sir Robert Smirke, famous for his British Museum and other fine buildings. He added the broad podium or base to the house, the elegant Ionic portico, and the flanking wings, to transform it into an excellent Greek Revival villa, this being the first time that this style had been used in West Yorkshire. The actual construction of the house owes much to the influence of Gott, for, like his mills, it incorporates substantial fireproofing features, including vaulted masonry floors supported on cast-iron beams, and a cast-iron back-stair, all of which made the house much safer than most others of this date.

Although lacking the scale of a great house, it more than made up for this by the richness of its contents. Paintings by artists such as Titian, Rubens, Caravaggio, Poussin, Canaletto, Veronese, Breughel and de Hooch lined its walls, along with a portrait of Benjamin Gott by Sir Thomas Lawrence. There was also a fine collection of modern sculpture, including portrait busts of James Watt and John Rennie by Chantrey, and of the Gott family by the sculptor Joseph Gott.

Standing on the east lawn, by the portico, there are magnificent views both up and down the Aire valley. Upstream, the route of the trail can be traced back to Kirkstall Abbey, while downstream it can be seen to follow the towpath past Armley Mills and on towards Leeds. As Repton noted in 1810, the mills 'can never fail to be an interesting object by daylight, and at night presents a most splendid illumination of gas light ...'

From the portico of Armley House, follow the path to the left of the lawn, by the edge of the woods, through which the canal can be seen, some 125ft below. Keep to the left,

Between 1810 and 1822 Benjamin Gott employed Sir Robert Smirke to transform the old red-brick house of the Woolrich family into this splendid Greek-revival villa. Behind its classical façade, Armley House employed the most modern forms of building technology, with a fireproof construction of cast-iron beams and brick arches.

down the steps and footpath, to cross the canal and rejoin the towpath at Redcote Bridge.

47. REDCOTE BRIDGE

Up to the early 20th century, Redcote was a small hamlet of picturesque farms, entered by a track coming down from Armley. This was called 't' Lantern Hoil', since workers used to light their way with lanterns when going to and from work at the nearby mills in the early morning and evening. The present bridge dates from 1821-3, when Benjamin Gott built a new drive from Armley House, across the canal, and across the river, to provide a convenient route across to Kirkstall Road. Originally there was a pair of lodges on the northern end of the bridge, but they were demolished many years ago.

Probably painted in the 1790s, this delightful watercolour by R.A. Riddell shows the old farm at Redcote Bridge. Other interesting features include Armley House on the hilltop to the left, and Kirkstall Abbey in the distance on the right.
Now turn downstream, towards Leeds.

48. KIRKSTALL POWER STATION WHARF

The next two concrete bridges carry the towpath over the entrances to a wharf built to receive boats which delivered their heavy loads of coal here from the pits downstream up to the 1960s. Kirkstall Power Station was designed and built by the City of Leeds between 1928 and 1930, its terracotta decoration featuring the City's arms, the eyes of their supporting owls being appropriately lit by electricity. Inside were three Stirling three-drum boilers, supplying steam to drive three B.T.H. turbine units, producing a total capacity of 80,000 kilowatts. Between 1943 and 1944 the station was extended to the north, four additional generators raising its output to 200,000 kilowatts. After further expansion in the late '40s and early '50s, it continued to provide power to the Leeds area until its closure in October 1978. The cooling towers were cleared the following year, and final demolition completed in 1986, removing a notable feature of the local landscape, but returning something of its original rural character.

The rural character of this section of the valley survived virtually intact up to 1928, when the City of Leeds built Kirkstall Power Station here. This photograph of 1944 shows the extended building from the north-east. Note the conveyor on the right, which brought coal from the canalside wharf, over the railway line, and into the boilerhouse.

49. PASTURE HILLS

The green hills overlooking the canal were still used for grazing dairy herds up to the 1850s, where, as a local poet proclaimed:

'Western breezes cheer thy meadow flowers,
And from thy 'Pasture Hills' are ever seen
The winding river and the Abbey towers ...'

By 1865 industrialisation had begun to intrude, one inspired visitor observing that:

'The green and variegated hills were shaded on one side by pleasant villas and clusters of trees, and on the other side gradually rose and stretched themselves into a vast perspective, the summits propping up the sky; yet, even here, tall chimneys sent up high curly masses of smoke, while in the distance large iron works continued to emit columns of fire to parody the sun with a lurid glare'.

50. THE LEEDS AND BRADFORD RAILWAY BRIDGE

This bridge, of the Pratt truss variety, carried the Leeds and Bradford Railway of 1846-7 over the canal. Note the numerous mason's marks on the stonework. There are crosses, diamonds, triangles, arrows, Stars of David, 'H's, and other marks, each indicating that they were the work of a particular individual.

On the downstream side of the bridge there are seats and a viewing area looking over the river. Below is Armley Mills weir, the noticeable kink in its otherwise smoothly-curving brim marking the point where it was damaged by bombing during the Second World War. On the fields opposite, now occupied by tailoring factories, the Royal Agricultural Show was held in 1861. A branch from the railway brought visitors to a station on the left bank of the river, from where they crossed a temporary bridge into the showground itself.

51. ARMLEY MILLS BRIDGE

One of the original canal bridges, it gave access both to Armley Mills, and to the river ford beyond, which led to Headingley, Burley and Leeds.

52. CANAL ROAD BRIDGE

This bridge was first built in 1882, when Canal Road was extended across the canal, and onto a viaduct which ran on the spit of land between the canal and the river, to thread its way under Kirkstall Viaduct and over the river to join Kirkstall Road. Before its construction, this route went across Armley Mills Canal Bridge, through the mill yard, to a ford leading to Milford Place (i.e mill - ford - place) to join an ancient trackway up to Headingley. Since 1882 a long staircase from the Canal Road Bridge pavement has led down to an iron footbridge close to the ford. This is the only point where, according to a local riddle, you can stand on a bridge, look under a bridge, look over a bridge, and still see the Town Hall clock!

The original Canal Road Bridge was of Pratt girder construction, designed by A.W. Morant of Leeds. This was replaced by the present concrete bridge in 1979, on which the fine cast-iron balustrade of the old bridge has been skilfully restored.

Here the trail divides. Either continue on the towpath towards Leeds (no. 54), or go up the steps at the side of the bridge, cross the canal, and walk down the drive parallel to the canal to the Armley Mills Museum.

Built in 1805-7 to serve the local domestic cloth industry, Armley Mills is a building of major importance. It is the oldest surviving example of the revolutionary form of fireproof construction incorporating hollow cast-iron columns, inverted T-section cast-iron beams, and floors composed of brick arches.

53. ARMLEY MILLS

Armley Mills occupy one of the best sites in the whole of the West Riding for harnessing water power, for here the Aire takes a sweeping curve around a flat rock-based plateau at the base of Dunkirk Hill.

Built shortly after the Dissolution, they were leased by Henry Savile to a Leeds clothier named Richard Booth, from whom they passed to the Casson and Moore families, a document of 1707 describing them as 'that fulling mill in Armley ... containing two wheels and four stocks with the mill house there

unto belonging ... also the water corn mill and all the fulling mills adjoining ... containing one wheel and two stocks'. Between 1722 and 1788 they were leased to John Walker, who installed very early scribbling machines here to prepare fleeces for spinning. In 1788 the mills were purchased by Thomas Lloyd, a leading Leeds cloth merchant, who completely redeveloped the site, cutting a new goit so that all the water from the river could be diverted to the wheels of this new fulling mill. Probably designed by John Sutcliffe of Halifax, it had 18 fulling stocks, a 'wool teaser', a 'wool plucker' and seven scribbling machines, making it the first major textile mill in Leeds. It was still not a factory, however, for its purpose was to serve the needs of the local handloom-weaving community, preparing their wool for spinning, and then fulling their woven cloth, thickening, felting and shrinking it ready for sale to the merchants in Leeds cloth halls.

A major corn mill was also built at this time, complete with an extensive kiln for drying oats, both the grain and the coal used for fuel being fed down chutes near the adjoining canal wharf to emerge on the relevant floors below. On 20th November 1805, despite the efforts of the local villagers and the Leeds Volunteers, the entire fulling mill was burnt to the ground, leaving only the corn mill and a warehouse intact.

At this time, the mills were in the process of being sold to Benjamin Gott, who now began the rebuilding. Since he had close personal experience of mill fires, he decided to adopt the latest

The wool textile gallery at Armley Mills illustrates the process of cloth making, from the arrival of the fleece to the baling of the finished cloth, using original machinery collected from local mills. Here the Jacquard and Hattersley standard looms are displayed in their authentic setting.

methods of fireproof construction, with cylindrical iron columns supporting inverted T-section cast-iron beams and shallow brick- arched stone floors. With the exception of the roof, the present building still stands in its original 1805-7 condition, now being the oldest surviving example of this revolutionary form of construction. Regrettably the two great water-wheels, each 28ft long by 18ft in diameter, apparently the first to be constructed on the suspension principle, were removed and replaced by a water turbine in 1888. A further innovation was the use of gas for lighting, a plant commissioned from Boulton and Watt being installed in 1809.

The Gott family continued to operate the mills as a woollen factory up to the 1860s, when they were leased to Kinnear, Holt & Co., yarn spinners, followed in the '80s and '90s by a variety of worsted and woollen coating manufacturers, milling machine makers, scribblers and spinners, size boilers, dyers and boot makers. From 1907 one of the previous tenants, Messrs Bentley & Tempest, became sole occupants, operating the mills for the production of a variety of woollen cloths up to 1969. Then, after four centuries of continuous involvement in the textile industry, it was purchased by the City Council to form a museum covering all aspects of Leeds' remarkable industrial heritage.

Armley Mills were opened to the public on 22nd May 1982, by BBC's *Blue Peter* team. Here visitors can see the whole process and development of the wool textile industry, the tailoring industry and the optics industry in a series of

authentic period settings, which were pioneered here and have achieved international awards. Further galleries show some of the museum's unique collection of printing machinery, machine tools, stationary engines, and, perhaps most impressive of all, its collection of mines, narrow and standard-gauge locomotives, all these products having been designed and made in Leeds. Whenever possible, and particularly during summertime public holidays, the machinery and engines can be seen at work, with the great 300-spindle spinning mules in action, the 1920s Armley Palace Picture House

In recent years Armley Mills has created a unique collection of Leeds-built railway locomotives, organising the return of significant engines from India, Chile etc. The museum's engineers restore them to the highest standards, as may be seen with 'Jack', the Hunslet Engine Company, narrow-gauge loco of 1898 which now runs on the Armley Mills Light Railway.

showing period films, the superbly restored mill engine in operation, or locomotives running on the Armley Mills Light Railway. This is a large museum with lots to see. At least two hours should be allowed for the visit.

54. BOTANY BAY

The former canal wharf on the opposite side of the canal, near Canal Road Bridge, was officially called Airegate Wharf. It is popularly known locally, however, as Botany Bay since, according to local tradition, the first load of wool imported from Australia was landed here in 1807, for spinning at Armley Mills.

55. THE LEEDS AND THIRSK RAILWAY VIADUCT

In 1844 George Hudson, 'the Railway King' was trying to funnel all railway traffic to the north and east through York. To avoid this situation, the wealthy industrialists of Leeds formed a committee to promote 'a cheaper, more expeditious and direct communication ... between Leeds and the Towns and Villages West thereof and the towns of Harrogate, Ripon ... Newcastle, Edinburgh and other parts of Scotland'. The committee obtained the necessary Act of Parliament on 21st June 1845, and began to construct the line the following September. Designed by Thomas Grainger, and built in the local Bramley Fall stone, the viaduct carries the line directly across the Aire valley, and on, through the Bramhope Tunnel, over the Wharfe Viaduct, to Harrogate and Knaresborough. The treatment of the canal arch is particularly attractive, entailing huge rusticated voussoirs in the

elliptical arch, and niches in the flanking abutments. It was completed on 23rd March 1849, the whole line opening on 9th July of that year.

In 1851 the line became the Leeds Northern Railway, amalgamating into the North Eastern in 1854, and the London North Eastern Railway in 1923.

The combination of Thomas Grainger's skilful designs and the quality of the local Bramley Fall stone ensured that the civil engineering works on the Leeds-Thirsk Railway of 1846 were of the highest standard. This fine arch of Kirkstall Viaduct bridges the trail and the canal just downstream from Armley Mills

56. GIANT'S HILL

Here stood a Norman castle, strongly sited on its steep hill overlooking the ford on the river below. In 1086 it was in the occupation of Ligulfr, followed by William de Reineville and Robert de Stapleton in 1166, and Roger de Leeds in the late 13th and early 14th centuries. Its main camp was over 100 ft in diameter, with banks over 20 ft in height, the bailey below being over 125ft square. As Ralph Thoresby recorded in 1715, it was 'commonly known by the Name of *Gyants - hill*; from whence the vulgar fancy I know not what Giant threw a Prodigious great Stone into a Lane a good distance on the North Side of the River, whereas this is upon the South Banks of it; upon which Stone the credulous can see the impressions of his Fingers'.

Giant's Hill was firstly damaged by the construction of the canal, then destroyed in 1874, when the Leeds Forge was built on the site. The stone, meanwhile, stood on the north side of Burley Road, close to its junction with Woodsley Road, until after the Second World War, when it was removed to facilitate re-paving.

57. THE LEEDS FORGE

The huge masonry foundations set into the bank on the opposite side of the canal, strongly built both with brick and with square blocks of iron slag, mark the site of the Leeds Forge. Founded by Samson Fox in 1874, it first

This steel first-class, day and sleeping bogie carriage was designed and made at Leeds Forge's Newlay works for the Lourenco Marques Railway, South Africa, in 1922.

manufactured best Yorkshire iron, but in 1883 it changed to Siemens-Martin open-hearth steel, producing up to 600 tons per week. In 1877 Samson Fox patented a corrugated boiler tube, which gave much greater steam-raising capacity to boilers, and enabled them to produce a much higher pressure. For this reason it was rapidly adopted for the warships

The rolling and pressing shop at Leeds Forge. Two of the corrugated boiler flues invented here can be seen in the centre of this photograph taken around 1900.

of the British and foreign navies, as well as for commercial cargo vessels and luxury liners. During the late 1880s the forge began to manufacture pressed steel under-frames and bogies for railway rolling stock, which soon became its major product, being exported for use in Australia, South Africa and India. Soon complete vehicles were being made, such as high-capacity waggons, bulk grain waggons and ballasting waggons, while from 1920 steel passenger carriages were made for European, Indian, Australian, African, Sudanese, Chinese, and Hong Kong railways. The company closed down in 1936, the site then being cleared, leaving it as it is seen today.

58. THE TANNERIES

From the 1820s, the land between Kirkstall Road and the river was developed as a major industrial site, with foundries, engineering and chemical works etc. Here too were Leeds' foremost tanneries.

Local hides had been tanned in small Leeds tanneries for centuries, but during the early 19th century the industry expanded rapidly to become the largest outside London. This was largely due to the rising population, which ate more meat, and hence produced both more hides and more demands for leather products, the improvement of the transport system, which could now import raw hides and export finished leathers to and from distant parts of the world, and the ability of the local engineering companies to produce industrial leatherworking machinery. A further factor was the building of Kirkstall Road in 1827, which gave access

to a number of flat riverside plots ideal for the building of large industrial tanneries. Within a short time this area at the opposite side of the river was one of Britain's major tanning centres, led by the following companies:

Joppa Tannery

This was the creation of Richard Nickols, the driving force of the tannery from its creation in 1828 up to the time of his death in 1879. He was largely responsible for introducing East India kips, small cattle or calf hides, into the Leeds tanning industry, and also for developing new methods of tanning. During the late nineteenth century the company, trading as Richard Nickol and Beckwith, occupied a four acre site here, much of this space being taken up with 500 stone-lined tanning pits seven feet square by six feet deep, in which the hides were hung in the tanning liquor. The main product was upper leathers, for the upper parts of shoes and boots, made from British cattle skins, East India kips, South American and other horse hides. Most of these went to supply the leatherworking industries in Northampton, Leicester, Norwich, Bristol, Walsall, London and Glasgow. Sheep leathers were also made here, up to 10,000 pelts per week being tanned for export to Europe and the United States.

Viaduct Tannery

In 1891 William Beckwith gave up his partnership at Joppa, and established a Viaduct Tannery, where he worked with his two sons.

This photograph shows just a few of the 500 stone-lined tan-pits at the Joppa Tannery, Kirkstall Road, in the early 20th century. Here the hides were hung in tanning liquor to convert them into leather to serve markets throughout Britain, Europe and the United States.

Oak Tannery

Built in 1876, this tannery was described as the most complete in the trade, its 5,000 sq. yds fronting Kirkstall Road with a splendid façade of massive masonry in the classic Italian style by Messrs Firth and Kendall of Idle. Its founder, William Paul had started his business in Armley in 1865 by currying kips from the Joppa tannery, later expanding to the Rockingham Leather Works in Woodhouse Lane before moving into his new Oak Tannery. Here he processed 20-30,000 hides and skins each year, both tanning them, and going on to complete the currying within the same building. Working with his brother-in-law, Samuel Haley of Thomas Haley & Co., the Bramley engineers, he effectively mechanised many of the labour-intensive finishing processes, such as levanting, glassing, embossing, graining and softening. This enabled him to produce the widest range of leathers, for shoe, harness and industrial use in this country, and throughout Europe, South America, the colonies and India.

The Paul family continued to operate the Oak Tannery up to 1968, when it closed due to the importation of subsidised upper leathers from the Irish Republic. Most of the buildings, except the Kirkstall Road frontage, were then demolished.

59. Spring Gardens Lock

This section of the canal runs along a sandstone scarp high above the river, giving fine views across the valley to the Headingley-Woodhouse ridge to the north. Ralph Thoresby described this stretch of the river in 1715; 'At the foot of this Hill runs the River Are; along the banks of which, from hence to the Town, is a most delicate pleasant Walk; The Water being so calm and smooth, that it can scarce be discerned to flow; and the Passage in so direct and straight a Line, as makes it resemble an artificial Canal'.

Here, around 1700, 'an House of Entertainment', presumably a banqueting house, was built by George Banister, Warden of the York Mint.

At Spring Gardens, the single-rise lock lifts the canal 9ft.

60. Yorkshire Chemicals

Thomas W. George moved his stuff dyeing and cloth finishing business here to Spring Gardens around 1825, his son Edward Sanderson George using the skills developed here to analyse and identify the spices used to preserve Leeds Museum's mummy of the Egyptian priest Natsef-Amun, when he was unwrapped in 1828.

The Georges went into partnership as Hammond & George between c. 1877-85, after which the plant, which now manufactured dyestuffs, passed to William Walker & Co., who joined the Yorkshire Dyeware and Chemical Company in 1900. Around 1967 Walker's name was dropped, and since 1971 it has formed part of Yorkshire

Chemicals. In the 1950s, the first British dyes for acrylic fibres were developed here. Other products included; dyes made from polyesters, acetates and nylons; leather dyes and chemicals; adhesives and other special chemicals. A major expansion in 1973-4 saw the construction of the present offices and laboratories on Kirkstall Road, and a dye standardisation unit, which lies along the north side of the river bank.

61. Greenwood & Batley's Albion Works

This firm, probably the most famous in Leeds, was founded in 1856 when Thomas Greenwood and John Batley left their employment at the Wellington Foundry, and set up their own business

Greenwood & Batley produced an amazing range of products, this advertisement promoting their oil mill machinery, which was widely used both in this country and in many parts of the Empire.

at premises in East Street. As these soon proved to be far too small, they moved on to the present site, between the canal and Armley Road, in 1859. By 1890 the site had expanded to cover eleven acres, with over 6.5 million sq. ft of workshops, 1,600 employees, its own electric power station and a branch line from the Great Northern Railway, which bridged the canal and gave access to each part of the works.

At first most of their business was in the design and manufacture of machine tools for making small arms and ammunition, then moving on to electrical generation equipment, silk and rope spinning machines, torpedoes, tramcars, oil, flour and general millwright plant, textile equipment, steam engines and pumps, machine tools for testing, minting, woodworking, cloth cutting and engineering, printing presses and sewing machines for both cloth and leather. These were being exported to India, Africa, Australia, Canada, Hong Kong, New Zealand, Malta, USA, Russia, Japan, France, Germany, Italy, Switzerland, Austria, Belgium, Czechoslovakia, Spain, Portugal, Sweden, Turkey, Denmark, Norway, Brazil, Hungary, China, Finland, Honolulu, Uruguay, Morocco, Egypt and Afghanistan by the end of the 19th century.

In the First World War Greenwood and Batley made vast quantities of armaments, including 'Experimental Machines EMK', some of the first tanks. Having made five very successful battery electric locos for the Mersey Tunnel project in 1927, the company began to develop a thriving electric locomotive

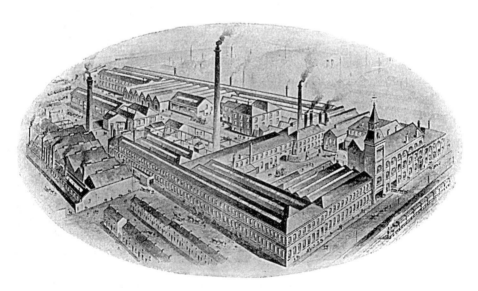

This aerial view taken from an early 20th-century Greenwood & Batley catalogue, gives a good impression of the size of their Albion Works. The trail follows the canal towpath shown at the top left.

trade, some 1,367 being exported to 40 different countries from this time up to 1980. These, together with a multiplicity of other products, such as mechanical handling plants, cold forging machinery, woven polypropylene sack plants, furnace chargers and specialised mining and coke car locomotives, ensured success up to May 1980, when as a result of a brief period of trading losses, the company was forced to close. The locomotive business and goodwill were acquired by Hunslet Holdings Ltd, who then administered the production of the famous 'Greenbat' range from their Jack Lane works.

The industrial buildings lining the southern bank of the canal, downstream from Greenwood & Batley's, and alongside Oddy's Lock, were used for a variety of purposes. Around 1900, for example, Leedham & Heaton's Armley Road Iron Works made spades, shovels and steel fenders here, the Leeds Wheel

& Axle Company made wheels etc. for railway rolling stock, and Canal Mills, formerly operated by Dixon, Robinson & Co., cloth manufacturers, was tenanted by a number of small textile firms.

62. ODDY'S LOCK

The lock-keepers house here, by the two-rise 13ft 7in lock, was originally a pair of single-storey cottages, converted to their present form in the late 19th century. On the wall opposite are a fine group of murals painted by Graeme Willson of the Yorkshire Mural Artists Group in 1981-4, on the theme of 'Fragments from the Post-Industrial State'.

63. CASTLETON MILLS

The first stone of Castleton Mills was laid on 20th August 1836, a 1½lb cannon ball found when digging the foundations probably coming from the Civil War battle for Leeds. Its builder, William Hargrave of St James' Lodge,

Greenwood & Batley made this electric loco for use at Priestman Collieries' Norwood coke works in 1946-7. Its purpose was to haul a 72ton coke car as it received cascades of red-hot coke discharged from the retorts.

Built in 1836, Castleton Mills were designed for flax-spinning, the engine house in the background providing the necessary power by means of a Fenton, Murray & Wood beam engine.

Woodhouse Lane, paid £30,000 for its erection, then installing a range of flax-spinning machinery supplied by Maclea and March, and a magnificent beam engine by Fenton, Murray and Wood. The firm, which traded as Hargrave Brothers, finished in 1853, the mill later being bought by Thomas Leuty & Co. who made linen here up to around 1935, when they transferred to wool textiles, which they continued up to 1979. The next company, B.Y. Clothes Ltd, clothing manufacturers, carried out a full restoration of the mill in 1986, at which time the 1850s weaving sheds on the opposite side of the main building were cleared. Today it remains a fine example of an early 19th century Leeds flax mill.

64. WELLINGTON ROAD BRIDGE

The modern concrete bridge over the canal replaces a typical stone-arched version constructed in 1818-19 at the instigation of Benjamin Gott, who wished to improve communications to his Bean Ing Mill from the south side of the river. This scheme crossed the River Aire by a handsome stone bridge with a 100 ft span designed by John Rennie and built at a cost of £7,000. Unfortunately this bridge is no longer visible, being considerably widened and re-decked both in 1873 and in the late 1970s.

65. THE LEEDS AND THIRSK RAILWAY

On the bank opposite the towpath are the Leeds and Thirsk railway workshops of around 1846, the forges being recognised by their tall chimneys, while the remainder of the building was used

J. Rhodes' Western Panoramic View of Leeds *of 1832 shows the Wellington Road bridges designed by John Rennie in 1818. The large bridge on the left crosses the river, while that on the right goes over the canal. The centre of this scene is dominated by Benjamin Gott's Bean Ing Mills, the world's first major integrated woollen factory.*

as fitting shops. Behind this block stand a contemporary railway roundhouse, and a crescent-shaped repair shop of around 1870. No comparable group of railway buildings now survives in this country.

The imposing stone bridge spanning the canal, beyond the lock, is an excellent

This magnificent bridge was designed by Thomas Grainger, to carry the Bradford, Huddersfield and Thirsk railway lines from the southern side of the valley, across the canal, and then on across the river, to the Central Station in Wellington Street.

60

example of Thomas Grainger's railway engineering, its sound proportions and tasteful balustrade would enable it to appear just as well in the parkland of a country house, as it does here in its urban industrial setting. Its purpose was to carry the Bradford, Thirsk and Huddersfield lines of 1846 into the former Central Station on Wellington Street, the massive stone piers just upstream being for a parallel line leading into the goods yard at ground level.

66. St Anne's Ing Lock

This single lock raises the canal by 4ft 5in.

67. Monk Bridge Iron Works

This factory, started in 1851 by Stephen Whitham of the Providence Foundry, Kirkstall, was acquired by James Kitson of the Airedale Foundry in 1854, for the manufacture of best Yorkshire iron, which was hammered and rolled into rolls, bars and plates for boilers etc. In

1882 the Siemens-Martin process was introduced on the southern side of Whitehall Road for the manufacture of steel, which was first welded in slabs of up to 4,000lb before being processed in the rolling mills. By the early 20th century the major products made here were best Yorkshire iron, crank and straight axles, boiler plates, bars, angles etc., and steel tyres, crank and straight axles, and wheel centres for the locomotive industry. The works finally closed in 1969.

68. Monk Bridge

This bridge received its name from the Monk-pits, the meadowland to the north of the river. The first bridge here was erected to the design of George Leather in 1827 to carry Whitehall Road, the major road from Halifax, into the centre of Leeds. Its river crossing was an extremely elegant bow-spring tied arch bridge made at the Bowling Iron Works near Bradford, with a traditional arched

Painted around 1850, this watercolour shows the original Monk Bridge designed by George Leather in 1827. Beyond, a simple wooden bridge provides a crossing for pedestrians while in the distance is Thomas Grainger's railway bridge of 1846.

The second Monk Bridge, built for the Borough of Leeds by its engineer, Thomas Hewson, opened in 1886. Its design incorporated the Leeds coat of arms, the shield appearing in cast-iron on the canal bridge to the left, while the parapet of the main river bridge to the right was lined with cast-iron owls.

stone bridge over the canal. By the 1880s these had proved totally inadequate to handle the increasing volume of traffic, and so the Borough Engineer, Thomas Hewson, was asked to design a replacement. The new Monk Bridge opened on 1st June 1886. Its main 109ft span across the river is of lattice girder construction, that over the canal being carried on cast-iron ribs. Since it was built by the corporation, the Leeds coat of arms was carved on the pavement side of each stone abutment, and cast into the ironwork of the canal bridge. Regrettably the long rows of cast-iron owls which originally perched on top of the ironwork all disappeared long ago.

69. THE CANAL WALL

The contract to build the wall running alongside the towpath from Spring Gardens Lock down to Office Lock, was advertised in the Leeds Mercury on 15th July 1777. Here, between Monk Bridge

and the railway bridge, it is seen in its original form.

From here there are good views of the city centre, including the spire of Holy Trinity, Boar Lane, in the distance.

70. THE RAILWAY BRIDGE

The first bridge here was built in 1846 to carry the Leeds and Bradford lines into Wellington Station, the present concrete bridge being part of the major City Station refurbishment of 1963-7.

71. THE GLOBE FOUNDRY

The buildings on the south side of the canal, just downstream from the railway bridge, formed part of Green and Jackson's Globe Works, where they made woodworking machinery from 1846. William Jackson continued the business here after the partnership broke up in the early 1860s, but moved to a new site on Crown Point Road *c.* 1880, in order to expand his business. By the 1890s over 6,000 of their combined morticing, boring and tennoning machines were in daily use, providing ample evidence for the popularity and practicality of their products.

William Towler was the next occupant of the Globe Works, where he produced general castings, girders, roofs, bridges and steam dryers and traps for industrial use. One of the company's specialities was 'The Yorkshireman', an industrial gas oven for baking and cooking, these being used by Jacob's Biscuits of Dublin and other major bakeries.

After Towler's had moved on, around 1900, parts of it were used for light industry, the most prominent being Symington's Printing and Cabinet Works, which made a variety of fancy boxes c. 1900- 35, and W.H. Turner's tobacco factory, where cigars were made from c. 1900 to the late 1960s.

72. TOWER WORKS

Over the roof tops, at the opposite side of the canal, rise the two red-brick Italian campaniles which give their name to Tower Works. The smaller tower with the octagonal top, a copy of the 12th-century campanile of the Palazzo del Comune in Verona, was built by Thomas Shaw in 1864 to serve as a chimney, while the larger tower, modelled on Giotto's campanile of 1334 at the Duomo in Florence, was built by William Bakewell in 1899 to act as a ventilation shaft, extracting the fine metal dusts produced by the grinding wheels used here.

The firm of T.R. Harding started to make cast-steel pins for the gills, combs, card-coverings etc. required for the textile industry, in 1829, but became established on this five-acre site in the early 1860s. Not only was this the largest factory of its kind in the world, but its classification for pin sizes, the Harding gauge, became the internationally

This attractive view, taken from the canal basin, shows the bridge over the entrance to Office Lock, the Leeds and Liverpool Canal Office of 1841, and the campaniles of Tower Works. That on the left is a ventilation tower based on Giotto's campanile in Florence, while that on the right is a chimney based on a camponile in Verona.

recognised standard. Having been incorporated as T.R. Harding & Son Ltd in 1892, it amalgamated with two other companies in 1895 to become Harding, Rhodes & Co. After operating here for almost 120 years, Tower Works finally closed in 1981.

In addition to making pins for the wool, flax, hemp and jute industries, the company also developed a series of industrial instruments, including the 'Ideal' counter, which could count either the number of items a machine was producing, or the length of its particular product, whether it be paper, leather etc. Their tachometer, or speed indicator, was also widely used on all types of marine and stationary engines, and on individual machines, where it enabled the number of items made in a given time to be closely monitored.

The head of this firm, Col. T.W. Harding, made enormous contributions to the civic and cultural life of late Victorian Leeds, virtually founding the City Art Gallery and presenting some of its best-known paintings, conceiving the scheme for City Square, and presenting its fine statues of the Black Prince, Dean Hook, Joseph Priestley, and their attendant ladies 'Morn' and 'Even', in addition to carrying out major improvements to Abbey House.

73. THE CANAL BASIN

This area, the terminus of the Leeds and Liverpool Canal, has been subject to many changes in its long history. Up to the late 18th century it was a pleasant open meadow, with a number of residences, such as Water Hall and

Buckrum House, and a stretch of riverbank suitable for fishing. The arrival of the canal brought an expanding trade in cloth, timber, stone, coal, grain and other merchandise, but the basin retained its rural atmosphere up to 1846, when the railways arrived on its northern bank. Among the features to be seen here are:

a. Office Lock

The original canal bridge over the lower end of the lock was rebuilt in 1841, the vermiculated rustication of its arch, and the parapets decorated with octagonal panels, being completely different from those of the 1770s. The building next to the bridge was erected at the same time, the words CANAL OFFICE over its door indicating its original function. The arches in the adjacent railway abutment gave access to workshops.

b. The Canal Basin

This basin was cut around 1820 to increase the capacity of the canal terminus. In 1845 it was extended northwards to the river, Monk Pits or Arches Lock now enabling boats to proceed upstream as far as Bean Ing Mills. In 1823, 1837 and 1839 there were proposals that the river should be made navigable as far as Armley Mills, but these came to nothing. Even so, this link proved very useful for vessels taking coal and other materials to the power station, soap works etc. which stood on the riverside upstream. In the mid-1980s the basin was reduced to its present length and access to the lock walled up, since it had not been used for many years.

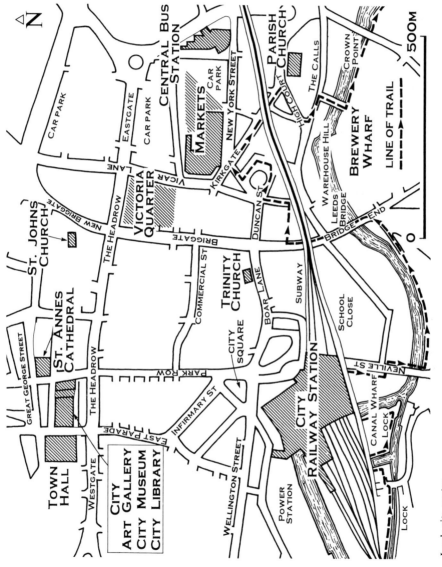

Leeds city centre

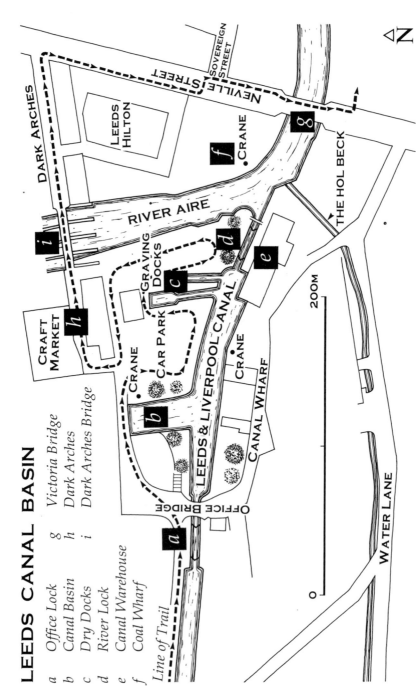

LEEDS CANAL BASIN

a   Office Lock
b   Canal Basin
c   Dry Docks
d   River Lock
e   Canal Warehouse
f   Coal Wharf

g   Victoria Bridge
h   Dark Arches
i   Dark Arches Bridge

Line of Trail

Leeds canal basin

The dock was also used for other purposes. In November 1823, for example, 'the Esquimoux Indian exhibited surprising feats in his canoe, which is made of seal skin and weighs 18lb, on the New Basin, where he gave the assembly convincing proof of the admirable dexterity of his countrymen. He heaved his darts, killed his game (6 ducks) and performed many other surprising feats!'

c. The Dry Docks

These two docks were used for the building, repair and maintenance of the boats. The upstream example, built shortly after 1790, has a wet dock giving access to a dry dock, which could be drained to leave the boat standing on supports ready to be graved, when its bottom would be cleaned and re-tarred. The downstream dry dock, meanwhile, was built shortly before 1820. Between here and the river William Rider & Co. operated a boatyard from 1863 to 1870, making and repairing the boats which

The canal basin's graving docks were used for maintaining the numerous barges which passed along the Leeds waterways. This photograph of the 1930s shows Leeds City Electricity Department's barge Wire No. 3 *being repaired in the 1790s wet dock, under the timber shed.*

plied the Leeds and Liverpool Canal and the Aire and Calder Navigation, including those which brought coal upstream to the Co-op. wharf and the power stations.

This area was also the main stone and slate depot for Leeds. When George Head visited this area in 1835 he found paving stones being cut by 'a machine at work for the purpose of sawing blocks of stone. It was driven by a steam engine [which] set in motion upwards of three dozen saws. The block to be cut was placed in a frame and moved horizontally, stone, frame and all, backwards and forwards by castors on iron rails. The saws, ordinary iron plates without teeth, were fixed immovably above the block. One boy attended all the saws with sand and water, adjusting, at the same time, by a screw-purchase, their contact and pressure on the stone.' In addition to paving slabs, local builders could find here all the supplies of building stones, slates and marble etc. required for their work.

d. River Lock

This marks the entrance to the canal from the River Aire. It has a lift of 11ft 3in at normal river level, and is deeper than the other canal locks, to enable coal boats to proceed upstream, through the basin and under the railway, to the former power station.

e. The Canal Warehouse

The large warehouse on the opposite side of the canal was built in 1777 to house goods for shipment along the canal, one branch of which enters its

The Leeds and Liverpool Canal warehouse stands beside River Lock, where barges left the Aire and entered the canal basin.

upstream end. It was open from 6am - 8pm in summer, and 8am - 6pm in winter, all candles having to be housed within a lantern as a fire precaution, according to the late 18th-century regulations. In the late 19th century, when it was mainly used as a granary, its interior wooden floors were replaced by brick vaults supported on cast-iron columns and beams to give it a much safer fireproof construction.

f. The Coal Wharf

The wharf on the opposite side of the river, near Victoria Bridge, was the town's main coal wharf. Here, George Head noted, 'the lighters, instead of bringing the coal in bulk, are furnished with iron tubs, like the keels of

From its first opening in the late 1770s, the canal basin became a major centre of the stone, slate and marble trade. Most evidence of this extensive business has now disappeared, but this advertisement of 1912 shows the great stacks of Yorkshire stone paving slabs which once occupied the southern wharf.

68

Sunderland. A lighter carried eighteen of these tubs, each of the latter containing 36cwt of coal, or one cart-load. A small steam engine is employed to raise the tub from the lighter to the wharf, a man, at the same time, hanging on the side of it, in order to knock out the bolt which confines the bottom, and thus let the coal fall into the cart'. During the 20th century this became the Co-op. Coal Wharf, with two mechanical railway-mounted cranes made by Booths of Rodley to unload the barges. One is now preserved at Armley Mills.

g. Victoria Bridge

A great flood in December 1837 swept away the timber bridge of 1829 which here linked Neville Street and Water Lane. It was therefore replaced with the present imposing structure, designed by George Leather jnr, engineer to the Aire and Calder Navigation, in 1837-9 at a cost of £8,000. Its simple elliptical arch, 80ft in span by 45ft wide, provides good examples of the huge building stones available from the quarries upstream. Since Queen Victoria had only recently

W.R. Robinson's watercolour of Victoria Bridge admirably captures the atmosphere of this busy riverside area in 1846. Note the man operating the crane at the far side of the bridge, and the paving stones stacked up on the wharf in the foreground.

been crowned, the bridge was named in her honour, her name being carved within a cartouche of laurel leaves on the central stone of the parapet.

h. The Dark Arches

This is the local name for the huge vaults which run beneath the railway viaduct. The northern section was built in 1846 to serve the terminal station of the Leeds and Bradford Railway. As the volume of traffic increased over the following years, it was realised that there had to be fast, efficient services between all the major towns. To solve these problems, the North Eastern Railway constructed, in 1866-9, an immense viaduct to link the former Leeds and Bradford lines with their Marsh Lane Station on the eastern side of Leeds, thus opening up through routes to Selby, York, and the north-east. The vaults under the viaduct, which now occupied the northern half of the canal company's property, were used for a variety of industrial and storage purposes. In 1892 supplies of tallow and oil in one store caught fire, causing enormous damage both to the vaults and to the bridge over Arches Lock, but the lines were back in use within a matter of days.

As a greater appreciation of the riverside area began to grow, the Dark Arches and the canal basin began to be substantially improved in the 1980s, one of the main innovations being the Granary Wharf Craft Arcade opened in December 1988. Here jewellers, designers, craft workers and importers of international exotica, and a café, are housed in attractive Victorian-style shops, while on Sunday mornings there is a bustling craft market

A popular Victorian ballad told the story of those who went Down by the Dark Arches beneath the Railway. *Today the Dark Arches lead to the attractive area of Granary Wharf, with its craft markets, cafés, shops and live entertainment. This section still retains its original drama, however, particularly where the river rushes through the cavernous vaults beneath the City Station.*

with street entertainment featuring anything from jugglers, fire-eaters and musicians, to historical re-enactment groups.

i. Dark Arches Bridge

This is one of Leeds' most dramatic locations, an iron road bridge over the river, all beneath the vast and cavernous arches of the railway viaduct. It is a scene worthy of Gustave Doré, especially in winter, when the river thunders through its echoing channels. As the *Leeds Mercury* reported in 1868, 'These arches extending over an area of at least seven acres, seem to ramble among the catacombs. Here one has the opportunity of observing the science of

arch building'. Upstream, the river can be seen flowing over the medieval Bondmans dam. In the 14th century it was being cleaned and repaired by tenants of the Manor of Leeds, who each received a rye loaf and two fishes for every day's work. From the dam, channels or goits carried water downstream to power a series of corn and fulling mills, which operated up to around 1900, when most of them were demolished and their watercourses filled in, ready for redevelopment.

When the water is low, it is still possible to see the Waterloo Ford, just downstream from the dam. Up to the opening of Victoria Bridge in 1839, this was the only heavy vehicular river crossing between Leeds Bridge and Armley. It was very dangerous, however, a horse and cart being swept off the ford in February 1823.

From the Dark Arches Bridge, walk away from Granary Wharf to its junction with Neville Street. City Square, City Station and the city centre are only a short distance to the left (north), but the trail continues to the right (south).

74. THE LEEDS HILTON

This modern hotel opened in April 1973 as the Dragonara, acquiring its present title in 1988, following Ladbroke's takeover of the Hilton chain. It occupies the site of Whitley's School Close woollen mills.

Cross Neville Street at the crossing at the Sovereign Street junction, and continue over Victoria Bridge (see 71g) before turning left (east) on the riverside walk.

75. ASDA HEADQUARTERS

In 1920 a group of West Riding dairy farmers came together to acquire wholesale and retail outlets for their daily produce. This had grown into Associated Dairies and Farm Stores by 1949, a public company with nine operating centres in Yorkshire, Durham and Northumberland, expansion continuing to 1965, when it became Asda Stores. Following visits to the United States, the directors became convinced that the future of shopping lay in huge superstores, where all household needs could be bought under one roof. Having adopted this policy, the company boomed, establishing over 100 superstores between Aberdeen and Plymouth, in which 50,000 people served over two million customers each week.

Asda headquarters

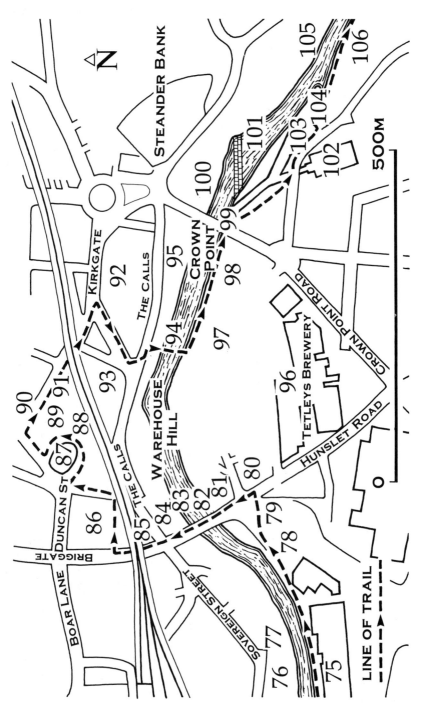

Detailed map of locations 75-106 in central Leeds

In the mid-1980s, Asda's headquarters in Kirkstall Road and seven other locations were proving unsatisfactory, and so it was decided that a new headquarters building should be built on this seven acre riverside site. This was a bold move, since this area was still considered by many to be nothing more than an area of industrial dereliction. In many ways, the new Asda building became a flagship of the redevelopment of the Leeds waterfront.

Designed by the John Brunton Partnership, the Asda headquarters of 1986-8 provided over 200,000ft of office space, its attractive brick exterior, with gabled slate roof, admirably reflecting the traditional riverside architecture of Leeds. Great care was also taken with its surroundings, which have numerous shrubs, trees, and this fine riverside walk.

"THE KING OF THE CRUET."

YORKSHIRE RELISH

The Most Delicious Sauce in the World.

Makes the Plainest Viands Palatable and the Daintiest Dishes more Delicious.
Enriches Soups, Stews, Chops, Steaks, Fish, &c.

Sold in Bottles, 6d., 1s., and 2s. each, of all Grocers, Stores, &c.
BEWARE OF SUBSTITUTES.

Sole Proprietors: GOODALL, BACKHOUSE & CO., LEEDS.

'Yorkshire Relish' was Goodall, Backhouse & Co's most popular product.

76. GOODALL, BACKHOUSE & CO.

During the early 19th century the developing factory system provided employment for thousands of women, who now had to combine their full-time jobs with their traditional role as mothers and housekeepers. Since they had far less time to spend on their domestic activities, there was a great demand for tasty foods which could be prepared with the minimum of time and trouble. This was largely satisfied by the products of Goodall, Backhouse & Co., manufacturing grocers, which included baking powder, egg powder, custard powder, blancmange powder, ginger beer powder, etc. and their celebrated 'Yorkshire Relish'. 'Unsurpassed as a sauce, piquant and appetising, and good alike for fish, flesh and fowl', it sold a remarkable six million bottles a year, which made it the most popular sauce in the world.

Their factory, which occupied the opposite bank of the river from 1853, was demolished around 1990 to make way for the new office developments.

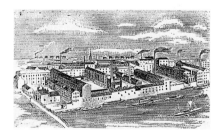

As this late Victorian wood engraving shows, Goodall, Backhouse & Co's works occupied an extensive area of the northern riverbank. Here they made numerous 'instant' foods to help working wives and mothers feed their large families.

77. Victoria Mills

These mills were built by the Victorian Ware Company in 1836, this date being seen at the top of the gable across the river. From the 1860s Victoria Mills were operated by Messrs Wild & Crossley, who traded as T. Crossley & Co., drysalters, logwood cutters, and dyeware manufacturers up to around 1901, when they passed to J. Crosland, and then to Appleyard & Co., who continued the business around 1906-10. In 1911 Hudson, Ward & Co. established their flour and provender business here.

An application for demolition was refused by the City Council in 1989, after which they were restored in the early 1990s, part being opened as the Leodis Restaurant.

78. The Old Red Lion

Dating from before 1809, this Georgian inn has an excellent contemporary carved red lion over its main door. After many years in private ownership, it passed into the hands of McQuat's, who had a brewery in Meadow Lane. In 1947 it was purchased by Samuel Smith's of Tadcaster, who continue to operate it today.

Continue along Water Lane, past the Georgian warehouse, to its junction with Meadow Lane, Hunslet Lane, and Hunslet Road. This area, just south of Leeds Bridge, was the site of the first Leeds Theatre, the Second White Cloth Hall, the South Market, and Salem Chapel. Its most prominent building today is:

79. Leeds Bridge House

John James Cousins, a Leeds banker, built this remarkable triangular block around 1880 as a temperance hotel, known variously as the 'People's Café' or 'Cobden's Temperance Hotel'. By 1900 it was empty, and was subsequently used as a dress and mantle makers, a dentists, and a manufacturing stationers up to 1910, when Tunstall & Co. Ltd, manufacturing chemists, moved in. In 1960 it was bought for demolition for road improvements by the City Council. Fortunately it was reprieved, refurbished, and re-occupied as offices in 1981.

Use the crossings here to cross to the east side of Bridge End, near its junction with Dock Street.

Leeds Bridge House clearly demonstrates how even the smallest and most awkwardly-shaped plots of land were utilised in late Victorian Leeds.

80. The Adelphi

There has been a public house on this site since before 1839, the present building being erected around 1900 by Alfred Bellhouse, the owner from 1889 to 1920. Later it passed through various hands, until acquired by the Melbourne Brewery, which became part of Tetley's in 1962. Behind the brick, stone and polished granite façade lies one of Leeds' finest pub interiors, with long upholstered benches, mahogany screens with superb etched glass panels, and walls hung with interesting photos, prints and documents. It is now designated as a Joshua Tetley Heritage Inn.

81. Aire and Calder Navigation Offices

The area between the river, Bridge End and Dock Street was occupied by William Milner's gardens and summer house in the early 18th century, but by the 1770s it was being built up as houses and warehouses. As the trade of the Aire and Calder Navigation increased, its terminus expanded from the north bank of the river across to the south, where a new basin was cut in 1821, warehouses were constructed both for the flyboat and for general goods, and other offices and workshops were built. By the end of the 19th century the Navigation decided that it needed more extensive and distinguished premises to reflect its position as Britain's most progressive inland waterway company, their new building at the junction of Dock Street and Bridge End becoming the head office of the Aire and Calder Navigation in 1906. Its badge, showing the arms of Leeds and Wakefield, the White Rose of

Yorkshire, a sailing boat, and the date 1698, is carved over the doorway.

82. 17 Bridge End

This shot of Leeds Bridge in October 1888, forms part of the first sequence of moving pictures ever taken with a single lens camera. The photographer, Louis le Prince, disappeared two years later in mysterious circumstances, leaving the lucrative field of cinematography to be developed by others.

In the 1830s this Georgian house on the downstream side of Leeds Bridge was occupied by James Hotham, retail linen draper. As a Quaker, he encouraged his house to be used for socially improving meetings, Elizabeth Fry, the Quaker philanthropist, addressing a meeting here on the subject of prison reform, while in 1847 Jabez Tunnicliffe founded that great teetotal movement, the Band of Hope, in the same premises. Following the removal of Hotham & Whiting in 1865, the shop was taken by Hick Brothers, ironmongers, tinners and sheet-metal workers, who erected a fine large teapot trade sign over their door, and continued to trade here for the following century.

It was from the upper floor of this shop that Louis le Prince photographed the first moving pictures using a single-lens camera in October 1888. He had come to Leeds in October 1866 at the invitation of his college friend, J.R. Whitley of Hunslet. After five years of development and research in America, he returned here in 1887, perfected his camera in 1888 and adopted the use of celluloid film in 1889. While on a train journey in France in 1890, he disappeared completely, probably due to foul play by one of his major competitors in the growing cinematograph industry.

83. LEEDS BRIDGE

In 1207 Ralph Paynel established a new manorial borough in Leeds, its enormous market place, now called Briggate, extending from the river up to the Headrow, the rows of houses down each side having gardens going back to Lands Lane to the west, and Vicar Lane to the east. According to local tradition, the river was then crossed by a ferry, with a ferry house where the Golden

Lion stands on the junction with Swinegate. There was certainly a bridge here in the late 14th century, supposedly built with stones taken from the ruined castle at the west end of Boar Lane.

It was here, around 2pm on 23rd January 1643, that Maitland's Parliamentary forces attacked from the south, driving the Royalist defenders of the bridge out of their positions, then continuing to attack the two sconces or breastworks at the north end of the bridge, which Sir William Savile had defended with two 9lb cannons. Although 'bullets flew about our men's ears as thick as hail', this manoeuvre, along with other attacks, proved successful, leaving Sir Thomas Fairfax in command of the town, its considerable supplies of arms and ammunition, and 500 prisoners.

The bridge was also used as a cloth market where the local clothiers displayed their cloth for sale on the parapets every Tuesday and Saturday morning up to 14th June 1684, when it was removed to Lower Briggate. The

This engraving of 1801 looks upstream, past Warehouse Hill, to the medieval Leeds Bridge, a stone-arched structure which was reputedly built with stone taken from the former castle on Bishopgate Street.

The new Leeds Bridge of 1871 was designed by T.D. Steel M.I.C.E. as a cast-iron structure with a 102ft 6in span. In the background, above the barge, is the Head Office of the Aire and Calder Navigation, now part of British Waterways.

inns around the bridge provided the clothiers with a refreshment called the Brig-shot, for which, as Celia Fiennes reported in 1698, 'any body that will goe and call for one tanckard of ale and a pint of wine and pay for these only, shall be set to a table to eate with 2 or 3 dishes of good meate and a dish of sweetmeats after ... I did only pay for 3 tankards of ale and what I eate and my servants was gratis [i.e. free]'.

To cope with the increasing volume of traffic, the bridge was widened in 1730, 1760 and 1796, eventually being demolished in 1871 to make way for the present structure. Designed by Mr T.D. Steel M.I.C.E. of Newport, in cast iron with wrought-iron girders and

cross-girders, it has a single arched span of 102ft 6in supporting a 60ft wide roadway. David Nichols of Leeds was the contractor, and the ironwork was produced, as at Kirkstall, by John Butler of Stanningley. It was opened on 9th July 1873.

From the bridge, there are good views downstream, both banks being lined with the former warehouses of the Aire and Calder Navigation terminus.

84. THE PITFALL

In 1695 one of the goits carrying water from Bondmans Dam (no. 73i) was used to power a water-wheel driven pump a short distance downstream from the north end of Leeds Bridge. This system, which replaced two earlier fulling mills, was designed by George Sorocold to pump water from the river up to a reservoir near St John's Church, from where a system of pipes distributed it to the houses of those who subscribed to the scheme. By 1835 the river had become extremely polluted, one writer describing 'O! ye gentle tea drinkers, the "azure tide" flowing placidly along, let what the sky will shine above it, impregnated with sundry other ingredients equally as palatable as the refuse of the dye- pan ...' Fortunately it went out of use in 1842, when a new supply was obtained from Eccup, to the north of Leeds.

Features of this mid-Victorian view downstream from Leeds Bridge include (left to right) W. Hirst's great Aire and Calder warehouses of 1827, a seven-storey warehouse of c. 1835, the parish church, the Crown Point Old Mills, and the old Flax Warehouse. Note the logger and his dog moving floating timbers in the foreground.

Continue up Briggate, crossing over The Calls, to the building just before (south) of the railway bridge.

85. THE TEMPLAR CROSS

As this property was owned by the Knights Templar in the 13th century, it enjoyed certain privileges, including the freedom not to grind its corn at the nearby King's Mill. To signify this right, the Old George Inn and the adjacent Georgian house which once stood here both had wrought-iron Templar crosses built into their walls. Following their demolition around 1933-4 one of the crosses was retrieved, and replaced in the present building. It may be seen just to the right of the central window at first floor level.

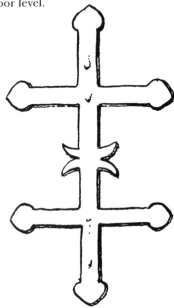

This Templar cross mounted on a building at the foot of Briggate shows that this property was owned by the Knights Templar in the 13th century

78

This archway leads from Briggate into Queen's Court, a rare survival of a house, counting house, workshop and warehouse of a prosperous Leeds cloth merchant of Queen Anne's reign.

Walk up hill, under the railway bridge of 1866 and turn into the first yard on the right (east) into:

86. QUEEN'S COURT

The large house adjacent to the railway bridge dates from the opening years of the 18th century, the courtyard, entered through its central passage-way, taking its name from Queen Anne. It was originally built as a major merchant's house, some of its first floor rooms once having fine pine panelling. The Oates family could buy their unfinished cloth from the market held just outside their front door in Briggate, then carrying out all the required finishing processes, baling and clerical work in the buildings surrounding the court, before despatching their goods to customers both in this country and overseas.

In the early 19th century, these premises were occupied by wool staplers, including William Hall, Isaac Wade, John Wood, Nathaniel Dixon, and Berendt & Levy, who bought fleeces, sorted them for particular purposes, and then sold the wool to weavers and manufacturers. During the late Victorian period the property was divided up into small units to accommodate numerous businesses, including a temperance hotel, a black beer and cordial manufacturer, a printer, a grocery warehouse and a tea warehouse.

By the 1970s, Queen's Court had acquired an unbelievably squalid appearance, many of its buildings being dilapidated or even burnt out, and the pavements heaped with rubbish. It could easily have been demolished at this time,

but instead it was then taken by Mr B. Prideaux, who carried out a complete restoration, thus preserving this unique example of an 18th-century Leeds wool-merchant's premises for the future. Here the Brigg-Shots restaurant takes its name from the traditional clothiers' meal.

Walk through Queen's Court, coming out at the other end into Call Lane. Cross this road, and turn up hill, past the White Swan, an old carrier's inn for the Batley, Dewsbury and Ossett area, to:

87. THE CORN EXCHANGE

For centuries, the Leeds corn market was held in the open air, at the upper end of Briggate, but in order to accommodate the growing trade, a Corn Exchange was built where New Briggate now extends from the Headrow. Opened in 1828 at a cost of £12,500 it offered facilities for the sale of corn by sample, warehouses and offices for the corn merchants, an hotel and four shops. After only 30 years, these facilities were totally inadequate, and so a competition was advertised for the design of a new Corn Exchange on an awkwardly-shaped plot between Call Lane and Cloth Hall Street. The winner was Cuthbert Brodrick, architect of Leeds' magnificent Town Hall of 1858.

In May 1861, the foundation stone of the new Corn Exchange was laid, the whole building opening for trade on 28th June in the following year, having cost £15,000 to build. Like the Town Hall, it was an extremely impressive achievement, its scale, form, bold detailing, and effective use of local stone making it one of the most memorable and monumental examples of Victorian architecture. From the outside, its oval plan gives it a sense of movement and interest which would be entirely lacking in a round building, these qualities being further enhanced by the fenestration, the diamond-pointed masonry, the sweeping cornice and the boldly projecting porticos, all inspired by Italian sources. The greatest surprise is yet to come, for the interior is never as dark and sombre as the exterior might suggest. Instead, there is a vast oval hall, surrounded by two storeys of offices and surmounted by a 75ft dome, its top and northern side having huge areas of glass which flood the whole area with natural light. This was not done for any aesthetic effect, but was specially designed to enable the grain samples to be viewed in the optimum conditions. As a contemporary writer commented, 'No roof that it has been our fortune to see has ever impressed us more than this one, as a work of original genius and thorough practical utility'.

In addition to fulfilling its original purpose, the Corn Exchange acted as a kind of giant village hall, being used for shows and events of every description. As a number of merchants attending the exchange began to reduce in the 1950s and '60s, many proposals were made for giving it a new permanent role in the City's life. In 1962 it was to be offices, in 1970 an exhibition centre, in 1972 a

The domed roof of the Corn Exchange was specifically designed to provide a flood of natural top and northern light which would enable the dealers to judge the quality of the grain samples in optimum conditions. In addition to this practical function, it is an impressive masterpiece of Victorian engineering.

concert hall, in 1975 a home for the Overlord Tapestry, in 1979 an antiques market, and finally, in 1986, a speciality shopping centre. In the meantime, its appearance had been maintained by cleaning the masonry as part of 'Operation Eyesore' in 1973, and carrying out major roof repairs. Even so, the £3m refurbishment programme announced by Speciality Shops of Knightsbridge in 1989 proved to be very timely, for much of the building required attention, especially as parts of the foundations were slipping into the early mine workings here. Since re-opening in 1990, the Corn Exchange has become a lively and colourful venue for relaxing in cafés or visiting numerous interesting shops, the gallery and basement storage areas now being made accessible by introducing new staircases etc. of appropriate design. It still functions as a Corn Exchange, however, the original wooden desks being used for trading

Leeds Corn Exchange is one of Britain's finest Victorian buildings. It was built in 1861-2 to the designs of Cuthbert Brodrick, the architect of Leeds Town Hall. Much of the corn brought up to Leeds along the waterways would have been purchased here by sample.

every Tuesday afternoon.

From the Corn Exchange, walk from Call Lane, down Cloth Hall Street, to the building with the pedimented roof and cupola, this is:

88. THE THIRD WHITE CLOTH HALL

Although the First White Cloth hall had been built for speciality cloths in 1710-11 (see no. 91), the open-air white cloth market in Briggate continued up to 1756, when the Second White Cloth Hall was opened to the south of Leeds Bridge. As this was rapidly outgrown, it had to be replaced by this building, the Third White Cloth Hall.

In the medieval period this area was an open field, which was purchased by the parish in 1555 with money left by Sir William Sheffield, so that its rent could support the master of the newly-founded Grammar School. For the next two centuries local weavers brought their cloth here to dry and stretch on tenter-frames after it had been wet-finished at the nearby fulling mills. When the white clothiers decided to buy this land in 1774 the purchase price of £300 was almost doubled by the £288 required for the necessary Act of Parliament. Work on site commenced in April 1775, and was completed in October 1776. It was a huge rectangular building, its 283ft by 166ft open courtyard being surrounded by, three single-storey and one double-storey, wings containing five 'streets' with 1,213 stalls arranged just as they used to be in the former Briggate cloth market. In 1786 William Johnson, agent of Lord Irwin at Temple Newsam received £14 19s 3d for taking down the

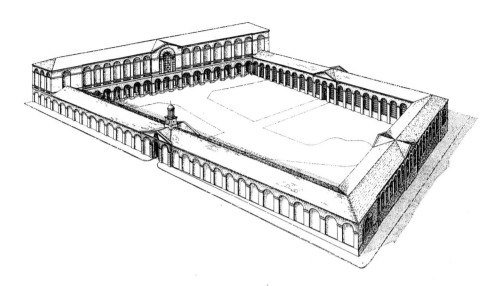

This reconstruction shows the Third White Cloth Hall as it appeared in 1777, with the entrance in its western side, and the Assembly Rooms over the northern 'street'. Today only these features remain, the other sections being demolished when the railway viaduct sliced through the site in the 1860s.

cupola of the Second White Cloth Hall, and re-erecting it here, where it held the bell which signalled the start and finish of the Tuesday morning markets. Many visitors to Leeds came to see these markets, for they were one of the commercial wonders of Georgian England. The white clothiers from the Ossett, Dewsbury, Batley, Mirfield, Cleckheaton, Bowling and Shipley areas, here 'lent over their bales of goods and lay hold of the merchants as they pass by, resembling importuning street traders, and I hear are as sharp in their dealings: such ranges of piercing eyes and importunate faces and voices I have not seen before' reported the artist John Russell in 1800.

The courtyard was mainly used for the delivery and collection of the cloth, but it also provided a very fine parade ground for the Leeds Volunteers throughout the Napoleonic wars, and for the exciting balloon ascents of Mr Lunardi in 1786 and Mr Green in 1823.

This activity all came to an end in 1864-5, however, when business was transferred to the Fourth White Cloth Hall in King Street. The North Eastern Railway drove its great brick viaduct diagonally through the hall, and new streets chopped through the remaining wings. The present section formed only a small part of the western side, which originally extended all the way from the Assembly Rooms to Call Lane. Over the following years it was used for various warehouse, workshop and lavatory purposes, before being beautifully restored by Speciality Shops in 1991.

After many years of industrial use, the gateway of the Third White Cloth Hall had fallen into a very poor state, but was then restored to its original splendour by Speciality Shops in 1991.

From the front of the White Cloth Hall walk up the hill to:

89. THE ASSEMBLY ROOMS

In 1775 the White Cloth Hall Committee decided to build Assembly Rooms for public entertainment over the north wing of their newly-opened building. They cost £2,500, this level of expenditure being due to their great size, 205ft by 33ft, and to their lavish interior decoration. In addition to the magnificent plasterwork, they were furnished with chandeliers, mirrors, curtains, seats, and girandole candle-stands. There were card rooms for gambling, kitchens and a supper room for refreshments, and the grand ballroom for dancing, concerts and other functions. They were the social

centre of Georgian Leeds, the major meeting place for the prosperous cloth merchant, professional and landed families, whose annually elected Master of Ceremonies supervised the entertainments during the October to March season. The Rooms first opened on 9th June 1777, with a grand ball led off with a minuet danced by Sir John Savile and the Countess of Effingham. As the following account of the Yorkshire Archers ball of 1780 shows, these were glittering occasions; 'The Ladies appeared in white, with green ornaments, and afforded the greatest display of taste and elegance. The ball was opened at nine o'clock by a minuet danced by the Earl Fitzwilliam and the Countess of Mexborough (patron and patroness of the society), deservedly admired by the whole company. Country dances commenced at ten, and the supper room was opened at 12 o'clock. It would be impossible to describe the decorations of the table ... The effect of the festoons of coloured lamps was

The Assembly Rooms of 1775-7 were used as a Working Men's Institute, a Christadelphian Hall, a hatters, printers, engineers, enamellers, butter importers, fireplace suppliers and a tobacconists between the 1860s and 1980s. This photograph shows it as it appeared around 1900.

The Leeds Assembly Rooms. 1777.

Described as the finest Assembly Rooms in the country, the Leeds rooms provided a magnificent setting for the lavish entertainments of the local merchants and gentry. The ballroom, seen here in its original state, was particularly elegant.

particularly pleasing. Dancing continued till three o'clock in the morning ...'

By the 1830s, tastes were changing, and it was reported that the Rooms had rarely been opened in recent years. Worse was to come, however, when the new railway viaduct sliced through the White Cloth Hall, and destroyed its former peace and elegance. In 1868 the Rooms were opened as the first Working Men's Institute in Leeds, offering washroom, canteen, games, library and reading room for local workers. The remainder of the building was divided up to house the Christadelphian Central

Hall, and premises for hatters, printers, engineers, enamellers, butter importers and fireplace suppliers. Having been purchased in 1919 for £8,500 by L. Hirst & Co., tobacconists, G.F. Bowman of Greek Street was commissioned to undertake their restoration as a tobacco showroom. He was responsible for removing the internal walls, and adding the new pediment and porch to the western end, the great Corinthian columns being removed in the 1930s, when a steel-framed mezzanine floor was inserted throughout the suite of assembly rooms.

In the late 1980s, the Leeds Assembly Rooms were acquired by Crown Exchange Construction Ltd, and converted into the Waterloo Antiques Centre, with dozens of interesting stalls and a café. There is also a small Museum of Georgian Leeds on the upper floor, amid the original rich capitals and fine plaster ceilings of the former ballroom.

From the Assembly Rooms walk round the north side of the Corn Exchange to Call Lane. Turn right to the junction with Kirkgate and then either turn left, and cross Kirkgate to visit the City Market or turn right to the First White Cloth Hall (no. 91)

90. THE CITY MARKETS

The land between Vicar Lane and Kirkgate was occupied by the Vicarage and Vicarage Croft up to 1822, when the traditional market for cows, pigs, vegetables and fruit moved here from their 600 year old location in Briggate, thus relieving great congestion and nuisance in the town's major thoroughfare. Over the following years, the market accommodation here was improved to meet the demands of Leeds' rapidly expanding population. The area was completely paved in 1827, and extended in 1846, while between 1853 and 1857 almost half its area was covered in a cast-iron and glass market

Within Leeming & Leeming's Flemish exterior stands the market's central hall, its fully glazed roof being supported by fine ironwork featuring the Leeds coat of arms. The central clock seen in this photograph of 1904 was removed to Oakwood when a new central entrance was made onto Vicar Lane.

The City Market's building of 1901-4 is a very impressive structure, its quality emphasising the continuing importance of Leeds as a regional market centre.

hall in the manner of the Crystal Palace, this additional accommodation enabling the Briggate market to be finally closed. Further extensions and new buildings to the east of the market hall were made in 1875 and 1888, a new wholesale fish market being added in 1894, and an abattoir and wholesale meat market in 1899. By this time the market hall had started to deteriorate, and it was decided that a much larger and more impressive structure was now required.

Following an architectural competition, the City Council adopted the designs of Messrs Leeming and Leeming for a new market hall, this being the present building, which was erected between 1901 and 1904. It is probably Britain's finest market building of this period, its Yorkshire stone exterior being designed

in a predominantly Flemish style, enriched by an impressive series of domes, pointed roofs and a high central flèche or lead-covered steeple. Inside, the great market hall was filled with cast-iron stalls, those round the perimeter having ornamental dragons supporting a wide balcony. Above this, a series of 24 cast-iron Corinthian columns supported a huge glass roof, its framework incorporating the City arms. The investment of a £$\frac{1}{4}$million pounds in market improvements since the 1820s proved to be extremely worthwhile, as trade continued to expand.

Despite being bombed during the Second World War, this expansion continued unabated, the markets being enlarged in the late 1940s, a new 'Tatters' market added in 1955, a new

Butcher's Row in 1956, and a new wholesale market on an out-of-town site in 1966. Now over 100,000 shoppers were coming into the market from Leeds and the surrounding area every Saturday. On 13th December 1975, disaster struck when two-thirds of the market buildings were destroyed by a huge fire. Fortunately the Edwardian market hall survived intact, replacements for the burnt-out sections being rebuilt in 1976 and 1981. In 1991-3 a joint £8 million project between the City Council and Norwich Union enabled the whole of the front section of the market to be fully restored to the highest standard, so that it still retains its position as one of Europe's finest and largest markets. Its 750 stalls, open from Monday to Saturday, with half-day closing on Wednesday afternoons, all give excellent value and are well worth a visit. It was here that Michael Marks first began his Penny Bazaar, which grew to become the great Marks & Spencer empire. In 1984 the company presented the clock under the central dome to commemorate the centenary of this event.

From either Call Lane or the City Markets, walk a short distance down to 98-100 Kirkgate:

91. THE FIRST WHITE CLOTH HALL

In August 1710, the Leeds merchants learned that their rivals in Wakefield were about to build a large hall to house their cloth market. Therefore, to protect and promote their trade, they obtained the site of a dilapidated almshouse here in Kirkgate, on which to erect their first White Cloth Hall. Ralph Thoresby described it as 'a stately *Hall* for *White*

Cloths erected at near a Thousand Pounds Charge by Certain Merchants and Tradesmen in Town; tis built upon Pillars and Arches in the form of an *Exchange*, with a Quadrangular Court within'. Inside there were 14 rooms arranged on two storeys, so that weavers from each of the attending hamlets could store their special cloths under cover until their own market opened on Tuesday afternoons with the ringing of 'the Bell in a beautiful Cupolo painted and gilt'.

This 'stately Hall *for* White Cloths*', the First White Cloth Hall, was built in 1710-11 to provide accommodation for the trade in special white woollen cloth. This drawing shows its probable appearance before it was divided up into 19th-century shop units.*

After being replaced by the later cloth halls, this building was converted into shops, the open end of its courtyard being blocked to give a continuous street frontage. It now awaits the careful and sympathetic restoration it so richly deserves, for in many ways this is the most important commercial building in the city. Its outstanding success guaranteed the rise of Leeds as the world's greatest wool textile centre, and created the wealth for its future industrial expansion.

Continue down Kirkgate, passing under the railway bridge of 1866, and crossing Wharf Street and High Court, to:

92. LEEDS PARISH CHURCH

It is probable that the first church on this site was built by Paulinus early in the 7th century. There was certainly a church here at the time of the Domesday survey, one which gradually developed into a very large and impressive central-towered structure by the mid-16th century. During the 18th and 19th centuries a variety of repairs and improvements were carried out, but a restoration project started in 1838 by the Rev. W.F. Hook, the Vicar of Leeds, resulted in the whole fabric being demolished and rebuilt in its present form by 1841.

R.D. Chantrell's design in the Decorated/Perpendicular Gothic style executed in Bramley Fall stone, gave Leeds one of the best churches of its period. It is the same size as its medieval predecessor, and is similar in appearance, except that its 140ft tower is now at the end of the north transept. Seating up to 2,000 people, it still serves as one of the spiritual centres for the city, many important events in the life of Leeds and beyond being marked by services here. It is, also, the only parish church which maintains full choral services throughout the whole week, its church music and choir having a world-wide reputation for excellence.

The interior of the parish church has innumerable features of interest, the following being selected to illustrate the history of Leeds and its waterfront, in the form of a clockwise walk.

a The North Entrance

Situated directly under the tower, this is the public entrance into the church. It houses a number of fine monuments to Leeds' major families, and a large

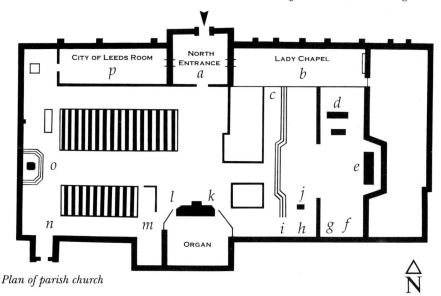

Plan of parish church

N

S. Peter's (Parish) Church from the River

PERCY ROBINSON DEL. 1894

In 1838-41 the medieval parish church was demolished and rebuilt in a uniform Decorated/Perpendicular style to the designs of Denis Chantrell, the prominent Leeds architect. The heavily-polluted atmosphere soon stained it jet black, but recent cleaning has revealed its original character.

As this photograph shows, the parish church is a very large and impressive building, the pews at ground and gallery level enabling 2,000 people to participate in its services.

diamond-shaped hatchment painted for the funeral of a member of the Beckett family. By the side of the door into the Lady Chapel is a memorial to Richard Oastler, the 'Factory King', who was born nearby in St Peter's Square in 1789.

b The Lady Chapel

Passing through the doors to the left (east), beneath the Georgian Royal Arms, is the Lady Chapel, where many of the monuments from the old church have been carefully preserved. They include memorials to many of Leeds' mayors, aldermen, merchants and cloth dressers of the 17th-19th centuries. Of particular note are those of; *West Wall* John Thoresby (*c.* 1592-1661) merchant, and father of Ralph Thoresby, the Leeds antiquary. *North Wall, eastern end,* Sir John Beckett (1743-1826) principal partner in the Leeds Bank of Beckett, Blayds & Co., which financed much of the industrial development of the town, and his son Christopher Beckett

(1777-1847), who continued the banking business and, like his father, was twice Mayor of Leeds. *South Wall, eastern end* Thomas Lloyd, (1750-1828) merchant, who rebuilt Armley Mills in 1788-90, and was Colonel of the Leeds Volunteers 1794-1807, *centre* Captain Lawrence Oates (1880-1912) of the ill-fated expedition to the South Pole. It was erected 'by his fellow citizens as a record of the brave act of "a very gallant gentleman"' in 1913.

c The Beecroft Memorial

The memorial at the north end of the chancel steps is to George Skirrow Beecroft (1809-1869) of Abbey House, a partner at Kirkstall Forge, and MP for Leeds 1857-68.

d The Hook Memorial

Dr W.F. Hook, the great reforming Vicar of Leeds from 1837 to 1850, built 21 churches, 27 schools and 23 vicarages in

91

the town. He is depicted here in a marble effigy by Keyworth; it lies on a red veined marble tomb designed by Sir George Gilbert Scott.

e The Altar-Piece and Sanctuary

The reredos above the altar shows Christ in glory, the walls behind depicting the apostles, being in glass mosaic work by Salviati of Venice.

f The Gott Memorial Window

The eastern window in the south aisle was erected to the memory of Benjamin Gott (1762-1840) of Armley House, and his wife Elizabeth (1767-1857). He was head of the West Riding textile industry, builder of Armley and Bean Ing Mills, a founder of the Philosophical & Literary Society and Mechanics' Institute, and a patron of the arts.

g The Thoresby Memorial

Beneath the gable of the original piscina rebuilt into the south wall, is the memorial of Ralph Thoresby FRS (1658-1725) a merchant trading with Hamburg, who developed a notable museum at his house in Kirkgate, and wrote *Ducatus Leodiensis*, the first major history of Leeds.

h Medieval Brasses and Effigy

On the wall below are the brasses of John Langton (d. 1459) and his wife Euphemia, of Farnley Hall, Leeds 12, and of Thomas Clarell, Vicar of Leeds (d. 1469). The stone effigy of a knight of the local Manston family dates from around 1325.

i The Hardwick Tomb

This altar tomb of 1577 was erected to the memory of Thomas Hardwick, Anne his wife, and their seven children, all of whom are depicted in oil paint within the recessed interior.

Monuments of this type are extremely rare, only about seven being known in this country.

j The Leeds Cross

Carved in the local Anglian style of the late 9th-early 10th centuries, the Leeds cross shows a mixture of both mythological and Christian motifs. It was probably erected to mark the grave of a local *thegn* or lord, then being cut up into blocks for building the late medieval church, and subsequently re-discovered and rebuilt by Chantrell during the works of 1838-41.

k The Organ

The organ is of international repute, the present instrument including pipework from the old church organ, with later additions by Hill, Schulze, Abbot and Smith, Harrison, and Wood Wordsworth. It is known to a wide public through the many broadcasts and recordings made here.

l The Pulpit

Measuring ten feet in height, so as to command the whole church, this fine piece of Victorian woodcarving depicts the Nativity, the Annunciation, and the Baptism of Christ.

m The Studdart-Kennedy Memorial Chapel

The Rev. Geoffrey Studdart Kennedy MC (1893-1929) was an army chaplain in the First World War, when he earned his nick-name of 'Woodbine Willie' for comforting wounded soldiers by giving them cigarettes. He was chaplain to King George V, and curate of this church and St Mary's, Quarry Hill.

n The Old Font

This was used from around 1500 to the time of Cromwell, when it was thrown out of the church. It came back into use between 1841 and 1886, when it was succeeded by:

o The New Font

Designed by Butterfield in 1886, this font stands on a platform of red, black and white marble steps, these colours signifying Christ's redemption, sin, and the redeemed.

p The City of Leeds Room

The north aisle of the church, the City of Leeds room, is a very attractive visitor centre, where refreshments are available on weekday lunchtimes and early afternoons, and souvenirs, recordings and publications on the church are on sale. Among its interesting features is the front of the Mayoral pew of 1660, with an early depiction of the Leeds arms, and the Penny Window, which was presented by the poorer members of the congregation in 1841.

On leaving the church, note the memorial across the road to Police Sergeant John Speed, who was killed in a shooting incident here on 31st October 1984.

Turn left, (west) past the grave of Sarah Crosby, the first woman Methodist preacher, and her companions, leave the churchyard, and walk along High Court to The Old Brewery, formerly Whitbread's beer and bottling store. On the right is:

93. LEEDS HERITAGE AND DESIGN CENTRE

Nos 17-19 Wharf Street were built as houses around 1860, and were converted into shops some 20 years later, no. 17 being connected with the Leeds slipper industry, and no. 19 a vets. After being used as George Shaw's dining rooms in the 1920s, and the Wharf Street vegetarian café in the 1980s, it has now been beautifully restored for its present purpose by Leeds Civic Trust.

The Trust is an independent, voluntary organisation whose members aim to encourage high standards of design, architecture and town planning, to help conserve and enhance the City's heritage, and to promote the improvement of public amenities and the quality of life in Leeds. The Trust set up Leeds Heritage and Design Centre here in 1993 to provide a facility where the public can come to see and hear about designs and projects for the enhancement of Leeds, and to discover more about the City's heritage. Its facilities include an exhibition room, a small shop and information centre, and the offices of the Trust.

From here, walk past 42 and 47 The Calls, and turn right (south) onto:

Opened in 1992, Leeds Development Corporation's new Calls bridge provides access to a large section of the south bank, and particularly to Tetley's Brewery Wharf.

94. THE CALLS FOOTBRIDGE

In order to improve pedestrian access between the north and south banks of the river, Leeds Development Corporation commissioned Ove Arup to design this elegant suspension bridge, which was opened by Michael Howard, Secretary for the Environment on November 18th 1992.

The centre of the bridge provides an excellent prospect of this section of the Waterfront. Looking around clockwise, Dock Street appears at the south end of the bridge, its north side being lined by the wide gables of the Leeds, Goole and Hull Transport Company's warehouses,

redeveloped as an attractive block of inner-city housing by Downes Illingworth & Partners for Barretts Urban Renewal Ltd, in 1987.

Next comes the Aire and Calder Navigation's basin of 1821, its footbridge being formed by a pair of huge trusses which supported a roof over this whole dock up to its recent redevelopment. Behind this bridge stands the 1826 Fly Boat warehouse, with its arched entrance for river craft.

Across the river, the northern bank was the original site of the Town's Warehouse, and an area known as Low Holland. The grey cement-rendered block was used in the late 19th-early 20th centuries by H.G. Atkinson, builders' merchant, who stocked Swedish laths, Welsh slates, Canadian pine doors, and all other related materials for local contractors. The next block, a large seven-storey warehouse, was built around 1835, and served as a corn merchants, a clothing manufacturers, and a wine and spirit importers, during its working life. Now, as Sparrow's Wharf, it accommodates an attractive riverside pub. Fletland Mills, the late 18th-early 19th century three-gabled block close to the north end of the footbridge, were occupied from 1887 to *c.* 1895 by Wright Brothers, corn millers, who ground flour and horse corn here for sale throughout the Leeds district. After being used for various other purposes, these premises have been completely refurbished as 42 The Calls, a 'deluxe hotel in miniature'. Next door, Brasserie Forty-Four opened as an international restaurant in 1991.

Downstream from the north end of the footbridge is The Design Innovation Centre. The building was erected in the 1930s as Spiller's grain and flour warehouse, later being used by Suma wholefood wholesalers, who made the top-rated peanut butter of 1986 on these premises. Alan Tod architects then prepared the present imaginative scheme for Yorkshire Design Services. The hoist towers were converted into glazed meeting rooms, while the warehouse interiors were transformed into design studios, exhibition spaces, and a resource and marketing centre for designers and their clients. It opened in October 1988. Next comes Langton's Wharf, Hillstar Developments' attractive

group of 67 apartments opened in 1991 on the site of a former stone wharf and coal staith.

95. THE CHANDLERS

Further downstream is the Chandlers, this area being formerly occupied by coal wharfs, the Crown Point Oil Mills, and the Corporation Sanitary Yard, on which the Crown Point Tramways Generation Station was built in 1896-7. The building at the end of the site, next to Crown Point Bridge, is William Turton's provender warehouse of 1876. This business, which supplied feed for horses and cows, had been founded in 1844, but by the 1890s Mr Turton had expanded it considerably, also operating as a major coal merchant from Crown Point Wharf, leasing the Newcastle-upon-Tyne, Gosforth, South Shields, Manchester and Salford tramways, and acting as chairman of the Bradford and the Leeds tramway companies. A local tradition states that he used the tall round minaret which rises above his warehouse as a look-out tower, from where he could see his vessels coming and going along the Navigation.

In 1987 the warehouse was incorporated into a new development of 120 flats designed by Denison Peters of Leeds.

At this point 'a long flight of steps, dark and ugly, descended between the houses, (the last being into the water) long known as Jenny White's Hole; and here.... Jenny White, finding "marriage vows as false as dicer's oaths", ended her unhappy life'.

Across the bridge, stands Tetley's Brewery.

The Tetley family had been operating as maltsters in Armley for 76 years when Joshua took over William Sykes' brewery in Salem Place, Hunslet Lane, in 1822. After making steady progress for several years, the brewery acquired the freehold of its site in 1864, and commenced a decade of rebuilding, with new offices, maltings, hop stores, Yorkshire Square fermenting vessels, cellarage and cask-washing sheds. This brought the capacity up to 160,000 barrels a year. Further developments in the 1890s included the formation of Tetley's as a limited company, the production of bottled beers and the acquisition of its first public house.

Now converted to hotel use, Fletland Mills were once used as a major corn mill. This Victorian woodcut shows the grain being unloaded from sailing barges moored alongside.

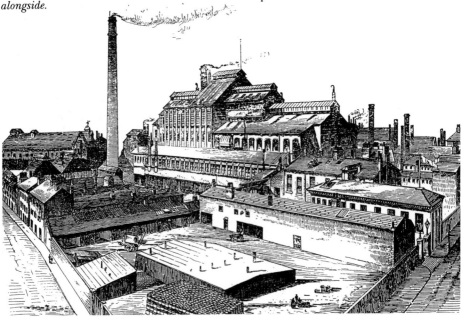

Tetley's have been brewing excellent beers in their Hunslet Lane brewery since 1822. Most of the buildings seen in this view of 1893 have now been replaced by efficient modern premises.

Continuing expansion boomed in the 1950s and '60s, when mergers with breweries in Sheffield, Bradford, Wakefield, Halifax, Malton and Warrington, combined with membership of Allied Breweries from 1961, brought a vast increase in trade. Renowned for the quality of its beers, production was expanded in 1986 by opening a new £10million computerised packaging plant, where casks are sorted, washed, filled, racked and loaded into the delivery fleet, and in 1989 a new £10million brewhouse for producing ale and lager. Tetley's have always played a very positive role in the life of Leeds, from actively supporting the Leeds Rifle volunteers in the 1850s, and the West Yorkshire Regiment, etc., to sponsoring a wide variety of sporting and cultural activities, including Yorkshire County Cricket Club and the West Yorkshire Playhouse.

97. TETLEY'S BREWERY WHARF

In 1993-4 the area of the former Corporation Cleansing Depot was completely redeveloped by Tetley's as a major visitor centre to tell the story of the English pub. Within the fine modern building, designed by Carey Jones Siefert of Leeds, visitors progress from a 15th-century brewery, through an Elizabethan inn, a 17th-century tavern, a Georgian inn, and Victorian and later pubs, all accurately recreated and populated by costumed interpreters to present a vivid impression of hostelries throughout the ages. This high-quality story is continued in the film theatre,

Tetley's Brewery Wharf is an exciting visitor centre on the south bank of the river. It tells the story of the English pub, houses the famous Tetley shire horses, and provides a full range of visitor facilities.

while on the ground floor the famous Tetley shire horses can be seen in their stables, along with their drays and harness. These attractions, and other facilities, make a great contribution both to the leisure and tourism scene in Leeds, and also to the regeneration of the Waterfront as a place where people can come and enjoy themselves.

From the Brewery Wharf, return to the towpath on the south side of the river, and walk down towards Crown Point Bridge. To the south stood:

98. BOWMAN LANE DYEWORKS

Founded in the late 18th century, this business was acquired by William Kitchen about 1860. It was one of Leeds' largest dye-houses, dyeing wool and cloth both for local companies, and for the uniforms worn by the army, the navy, and the railways.

99. CROWN POINT BRIDGE

In W.R. Robinson's 1848 watercolour of Crown Point Bridge, the chimneys of Bowman Lane Dyeworks and the Crown Point Oil Mills dominate the skyline, along with the tower of the parish church.

On 14th April 1840, an Act was obtained for the building of a new bridge across the River Aire at 'a place called Crown Point', its purpose being to relieve the growing pressure on Leeds Bridge by providing an alternative river crossing at the eastern end of central Leeds. Shortly after this, the 120ft wide, single-span iron bridge began to be constructed, with castings made at the Parks Iron Works in Sheffield, its designers, George Leather & Son, providing it with an elegant Gothic parapet and other detailing. It opened in July 1842, having cost some £36,000 to complete. Originally a toll was charged, but this was abolished in March 1868.

100. THE STEANDER

The area north of the river is called 'steander' indicating low-lying riverside fields. Here, on July 18th 1730, Abraham Powell 'was brought hither by the Sheriff's Officers and is said to have the sentence [of death] executed upon him on the common steander'. His crime was to have stolen cloth that was stretching on the unprotected tenter-frames, his public punishment being designed to act as a severe deterrent.

In the 19th century this area was occupied by three different businesses. First came the coal staiths, where in 1845 George Head saw how 'the coal is raised upon the wharf, 7 or 8ft above the river, by a simple hand-crane, worked by a couple of men at a windlass, it having previously been thrown from the lighter into an iron tub by men with shovels, which tub is raised, swung round over the cart to be laden, and emptied into it'.

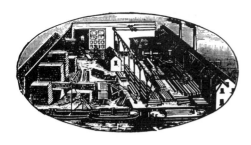

Scupham & Sons' Crown Point Wharf was provided with a travelling crane which could efficiently raise balks of timber from the barges into stacks, and then on to the saw.

The middle plot was a timber yard, operated by W. Scupham & Sons and then by Hudson & Co., where logs of partridge, zebra, zericote, cocoa, canary, sequoia, ebony, boxwood and other less exotic timbers were imported and sawn into planks for the local furniture and building trades.

The third plot was used jointly by B.C. Parry's coal and sand wharf, and the Crown Point Dye Works. William Brayshaw & Sons started dyeing here in the early 19th century, concentrating on black broadcloths, table covers, saddle cloths and uniform cloths. They also dyed the ruby curtains for Queen Victoria's apartments at Windsor Castle, in 1849 and 1889. Trading as J.C. Waddington from around 1900, the works dyed khaki and navy blue for the 1914-18 war, but were closed down by the Board of Trade in 1942, as part of a reduction in the number of Leeds dye-houses.

101. Leeds Dam

The dam probably has medieval origins, although there is no evidence of Nether

In this detail from Francis Place's Prospect of Leeds *of 1715 Nether Mills can be seen at the end of Leeds Dam, while just a short distance downstream is the original Leeds Lock.*

Built around 1840, the New Basin, or Clarence Dock, greatly increased the capacity of the Aire and Calder Navigation's terminus, depots for stone, timber, coal, lime and other goods soon being erected around its wharfs. Latterly it became known as the potato dock, since this was a common cargo here, while the Co-op. coal boats were moored here ready for unloading, until that trade ended in 1975.

Standing at the northern end of Leeds Dam, Nether Mills manufactured textiles, chemicals and dyestuffs up to the time of its demolition in 1957.

In 1990 the last commercial freight operator to use the Leeds Waterways, the Sellers family's Sand & Gravel (Leeds), had to move out of Clarence Dock when their premises were compulsorily purchased by Leeds Development Corporation. Fortunately they were able to relocate to a new wharf near Hunslet Mills, where they currently handle contracts for, up to 40,000 tons of building materials, thus demonstrating the value of the waterways for reducing heavy traffic on the roads.

Mills, which stood on its northern end, and was powered by it, until 1636. In 1715 there were two fulling mills here, and by the late 18th century the five water-wheels were operating nine fulling stocks, five scribbling machines, a number of cotton spinning frames, and mills for grinding dyestuffs. Its owner, Mr Fearn, gave his name to the land downstream, between the river and Timble Beck, which is still called Fearn's Island. From before 1817 up to around 1840, John Lee used the mills to manufacture carpets, Brussels woollen and cotton coverlets, and to scribble and slub wool ready for spinning. Then, for the last 80 years of its life, it was occupied by James Richardson & Co. manufacturing chemists, up to its demolition in 1957. Although plans were made to preserve its cast-iron water-wheel, it does not appear to have survived.

Walk up the roadway to the south, onto the bridge overlooking:

103. THE ROYAL ARMOURIES

Plans have now been prepared for the complete redevelopment of Clarence Docks, the centrepiece of this scheme being an imaginative new museum to house the world-famous Royal Armouries from the Tower of London.

The new museum will tell the story of the development and use of arms and armour around the world up to the present day. In order to explain the collections, and bring them to life for the public, the displays will incorporate the latest audio-visual techniques as well as

This view shows how the proposed Royal Armouries building will appear when seen across Clarence Dock.

live presentations by interpreters, demonstrations of craft and weapon-handling skills. The visiting public will also be given the opportunity to handle parts of the collection and accurate replicas.

Outside will be a large area for re-enactments of jousting, military drill, falconry and dog-handling skills. Next to this will be stables, kennels and mews for the animals, and a Craft Court where relevant craftsmen can be seen working at their trades.

The building itself is being designed as the centre-piece of the redevelopment of the entire Clarence Dock area of Leeds. It sits between the River Aire and the outer dock basin so that it can take full advantage of the surrounding water. It is intended to be a friendly and welcoming building. To achieve this, a public street

runs through the heart of the museum. This gives a foretaste of the excitement of the museum as a whole. It also allows the general public to make use of the main shops and restaurant of the museum, and provides Leeds with a major evening event and entertainment space for up to 500 people.

From the bridge, walk a short distance along Clarence Road, and through the gates, back onto the towpath:

104. LEEDS LOCK

The dam caused a major obstruction to the passage of barges, one of the Navigation's first acts being to construct a pound lock here, so that vessels could proceed upstream to the warehouses near Leeds Bridge. On the advice of John Rennie, the lock was rebuilt in 1822. It is still manually operated, being the only lock operated in this way between Leeds and the sea, the others having been electrified.

105. BANK MILLS

This impressive group of red-brick mills lines the northern side of the river, just downstream from Leeds Lock.

The first major six-storey block of 21 bays is B mill of 1831-2, designed for Hives & Atkinson by John Clark of Edinburgh. Its staircase and hoist tower project above the roof at the eastern end as a large circular turret. Beyond this extends D mill of four storeys and nine bays, which was added in 1856. At the end of this block Timble Beck enters the river, having flowed down from Golden Acre Park, Adel, Meanwood and Sheepscar, where for centuries it · powered corn mills, textile mills and

tanneries.

The next block downstream, standing back from the river bank, is the four-storey, seven-bay yarn warehouse of 1824, which adjoins the six-storey, 16-bay C mill of 1832-3, followed by the projecting six-storey, eight-bay tow warehouse of the same date, which has taking-in doors on each floor, so that cargoes could be unloaded directly from boats moored below. This, too, was designed by John Clark.

In 1791 the Leeds merchants Markland, Cookson and Fawcet built a cotton spinning mill on this site, its designer being John Sutcliffe of Halifax, who had only recently completed the new Armley Mills for Thomas Lloyd. Originally it was powered by a 14ft water-wheel on Timble Beck, but this was replaced in 1792 by a 30 h.p. beam engine by

Charles Cope's 1826 engraving of Leeds gives a good impression of its infamous smoky atmosphere. Leeds Lock and Leeds Dam appear upstream, while to the right, by the entrance to Timble Beck, is the first Bank Mills.

Boulton & Watt. The mills continued to spin cotton up to 1797, and wool for their carpet and worsted factories, until sometime before 1819. Shortly afterwards, in 1823, the mills were acquired by Hives & Atkinson, former partners of John Marshall of Holbeck. Although a fire of 1824 destroyed the original mills, new mills of fireproof construction were erected to the designs of John Clark of Edinburgh in 1824, 1831-2, and 1832-3 to accommodate their booming flax-spinning business. About this time some 550 hands were employed here, this figure rising to 12-1400 in 1867, when the firm changed its name to Hives & Tennant.

Following the collapse of this company in 1882, the mills were sold by auction, part being purchased by Roberts Mart & Co. for £9,500, the remainder being acquired in 1898 for £5,500. William Roberts had founded this company in 1852, when he began to sell paper and to produce print and packaging materials using a steam-powered press and a bag-making machine. Having entered into partnership with William Mart, he acquired Bank Mills and built a new extension to provide the accommodation needed for his expanding business. Roberts Mart continue to flourish as makers and marketers of a wide variety of packaging, including paper and polythene wrappings and carrier bags etc. for supermarkets and white products manufacturers, garment covers for laundries, and the contract printing of letterheads, leaflets, calendars, labels and food wrappers.

As with many other large mills, various sections were used for other industrial purposes, cabinet making in C mill being represented by James Conyers c. 1886-1905, Margolin & Sons c. 1900 and Marsh, Jones & Cribb in the 1920s. In addition, the corn millers Henry Leetham & Sons, were here c. 1904-1930, Catlow & Co. fruit preservers c. 1905-10, the Worth Manufacturing Company, skirtmakers, c. 1907-14, Dixon & Gaunt, wholesale clothiers, c. 1933-61, and Chadwick & Lunt, waste paper merchants, c. 1915-29.

106. THE CITY SAW MILLS

These stood on the south side of the river, opposite Bank Mills.

In 1833 William Illingworth of Roundhay Grove established a saw mill on Crown Point Wharf, where he brought West Indian hardwood logs along the Leeds and Liverpool Canal from Liverpool docks for conversion into planks etc. for the local furniture and building industries. Later he took Samuel Ingham of Headingley Hall into partnership, the firm becoming a limited company in 1900. Although the business was

Today Bank Mills form one of Yorkshire's most impressive groups of textile mills. They chiefly date from the period 1824-56.

operated from Queen Street Saw Mills during the late 19th century, it returned to this Clarence Road site in 1921, when a major saw mill was built here, fully equipped with the log-cutting saws, moulding machines etc. required to efficiently process the various timbers. American canary wood, satinwood and black walnut, African and West Indian hardwoods, and Austrian (later Japanese) oak were used by the local furniture manufacturers, Burmese teak was made into prams, Swedish, Finnish and Russian pine was used for the building trade, while Canadian yellow pine was used by engineers for model making. The company also manufactured furniture, especially desks for school use.

By the 1970s Illingworth & Ingham had diversified into do-it-yourself supplies, building materials, furnishing ironmongery and tools, many of which were supplied by the Montague L. Meyer Group, who took over the company around 1974. After almost 150 years of continuous activity on this site, it was finally vacated around 1981.

The southern end of the City Saw Mills was the parish church's cricket and football ground during the late Victorian period.

107. ST SAVIOUR'S CHURCH

St Saviour's lies on Cavalier Hill, just downstream from Bank Mills.

By the 1840s the Bank, the rising ground to the north of the river, had a population of 12,000 people occupying an area of only 40 acres. It was then 'intersected with courts which never seem to have seen the light of day, dirty and filled with inhabitants smelling of tobacco and rum ... proverbial for their filthiness'. Here 'the young of both sexes would meet after the day's work was over, and up to late hours of the night, coarse oaths and blasphemies might be heard in the streets, and revolting sights be witnessed by passers-by ... No decent person could pass through the chief street without being liable to gross personal insult'. Cholera was rife, atheism openly taught, and, on one occasion, a bible and prayer book were burnt in the street before a sympathetic crowd.

St Saviour's church stands on Cavalier Hill, dominating the surrounding Bank area, and the riverside. It was built to the designs of J.M. Derick in 1842-5.

In this unpromising setting the Rev. Hook, Vicar of Leeds, established the church of St Saviour, which overlooks

104

this section of the Waterfront. Dr Pusey, leader of the Church of England's Oxford Movement, informed Hook that he could produce the funds for a new church here, ostensibly from an anonymous donor, but most probably from his own resources. At first it was planned to ship in a genuine medieval church from Portugal, via the Navigation, but instead J.M. Derick was commissioned to design St Saviour's, which was built in 1842-5. The church marked a return to the medieval arrangement of nave, chancel and transepts, with a central tower which was intended to carry a noble spire, all in 14th-century Gothic. Its fine interior featured excellent carved woodwork, and fine stained glass designed by Pugin and by Morris & Co.

On 19th October 1935 a severe gale destroyed the church's temporary wooden spire, and damaged the adjacent roofs. Temporary repairs were made immediately, but then Mr Samuel Smith, a former pupil of St Saviour's School, provided funds to build the present tower in 1936-7, the foundations having proved too weak to carry the intended spire.

108. The Victoria Chemical Works

It is probable that Sayner's dyehouse stood on the south side of the river in the 1830s, but in 1847 William Armitage started a timber yard here, powering his saws etc. with a Fenton, Murray and Wood beam engine. His manager, John North, continued the business up to the time of his death in 1881, when he was succeeded by his son, Wesley North. The

chemical works, started in 1860, were relatively short-lived, but Wesley North & Co.'s saw mills were still active here up to around 1959.

109. The Clarence Ironworks

Taylor Brothers' ironworks began making best Yorkshire iron here in 1856, later installing a Siemens acid steel plant. By 1912, it was forging steel into guns, crank shafts, piston and connecting rods, propeller shafts, locomotive and waggon axles etc., as well as making air-vessels for torpedoes in carbon, nickel, and nickel-chrome steels. In 1921, the company announced its intention to move to Manchester, where it could supply the Metropolitan Carriage & Waggon Company, and enjoy better transport facilities on the Manchester Ship Canal.

110. Airedale Mills

Benjamin Vickers began his business career as an agent for London and Liverpool oil and soap merchants in 1828, later moving into indigo, seeds, bark and Baltic produce, and eventually going on to manufacture dyestuffs in 1858. As trade expanded, Airedale Mills were purchased in 1877 for the purpose of processing vegetable and mineral oils and grease for industrial use. Their products, which included non-corrosive engine oil, heavy wool oil and improved lubrication systems received international acclaim, and were exported throughout the world. Research and development has continued in the 20th century, especially in producing specialised oils for wool, silk, rayon and other man-made fibre processes. New laboratories and a works administrative block were opened in 1969, and the adjacent engineering workshops acquired in 1971 to provide blending and storage areas. Today, Benjamin R. Vickers & Sons Ltd, continue to operate as one of Britain's major specialist oil producers at Airedale Mills.

111. ST HILDA'S CHURCH

The tall red-brick church seen to the north of the river is St Hilda's, built to the designs of J.T. Micklethwaite in 1876-81, with additional vicarage, parish rooms and schools erected in 1892. Its relatively plain exterior belies the richness of its furnishings, which include a 41ft high rood screen carved by W.H. Wood of Newcastle, fine stained glass, a marble font, and a large painted and gilded pulpit.

112. AIRE BANK SAW MILL

The first factory to be built on the site just upstream from the bridge was Henry Hadfield's Aire Bank Saw Mill of around 1895. This timber merchant and packing case manufacturer, who specialised in mineral water and beer cases, closed around 1950.

HENRY HADFIELD,
Box & Packing Case Maker.
CRATES, BOXES & TRAYS of every description.
Speciality: MINERAL WATER & BEER CASES.
Airebank Sawmills,
LEEDS.
Telephone: 1034 Central.
Telegrams: "PACKING," LEEDS.

113. SOUTH ACCOMMODATION ROAD BRIDGE

As the volume of traffic entering the centre of Leeds began to cause even more congestion, it was decided that a new turnpike road should be built to provide an effective eastern by-pass. It was to commence on the main Leeds-Wakefield road in Hunslet, then cross the river and proceed to the main York and Selby roads further north. Having obtained the required Act of Parliament on 23rd May 1828, a fine iron bridge, with its roadway suspended from great arched beams, was constructed to the designs of George Leather. It cost £4,200.

The South Accommodation Road Bridge seen here was designed by Thomas Hewson, the City Engineer, whose department took this photograph on its completion in 1899. Note the temporary wooden bridge in the background.

By 1898 it had proved inadequate to handle the great numbers of vehicles which needed to cross it each day, and so it was replaced by the present lattice girder bridge, designed by Thomas Hewson, the City Engineer, in 1899. It has a clear span of 146ft, and is 50ft wide.

Ascend the steps at the side of the stone abutment, turning right at pavement level, to cross the bridge to the northern bank. Turn right here, and follow the path along the top of the sloping riverbank, continuing in front of the modern industrial units which occupy the site of the former Hunslet

Goods Station. This section of path, running between South Accommodation Road and the next river crossing was completed by Leeds City Council in 1993.

114. AIRE BANK

The plots on the opposite (south) side of the river were developed for a variety of industrial purposes from the mid-19th century. Just downstream from the bridge stood Isaac Dodgshun's Aire Bank Woollen Mills. Dodgshun started as a Leeds wool stapler in Basinghall Street in the early 1830s, importing wool for sale alongside the locally produced flocks, shoddy and mungo required for the woollen industry. Around 1875 his company began to manufacture woollen cloth here, continuing up to around 1950. Having been acquired by the West Yorkshire Metropolitan County Council, these mills were demolished in 1985 to make way for future inner ring-road improvements.

The adjacent plot was developed by Hirst, Brooke & Hirst, as a chemical plant. In the 1850s Benjamin Hirst appears to have gone into partnership with the Brooke family, who were chemists in Trinity Street, to form a company which manufactured chemicals, paints, colours and British wines, in addition to operating as wholesale druggists, oil merchants and drysalters. Their factory continued working here up to around 1900, when they removed to East Street. In later years Bryant & May, the match manufacturers, had their Leeds base here.

115. HUNSLET MILLS

The vast seven-storey, 25-bay mill building which dramatically dominates this area of South Leeds forms the major block of Hunslet Mills, an eight-acre flax-spinning factory established here by J. Wilkinson in 1838. It is a structure of considerable importance, not only in landscape terms, but also for its method of fireproof construction. Inside, three longitudinal rows of cast-iron columns carry early examples of 'I' section cast-iron beams, which in turn support fireproof masonry floors. This arrangement was probably designed by Fairbairn of Manchester.

In their early years the mills were beset by troubles of every description, a strike in 1847, severe gale damage in 1850, a serious cholera outbreak in 1854, the death of J. Wilkinson in 1855, two major fires in 1865 and 1866, followed by the bankruptcy of the firm in 1867. Despite these setbacks, it had made considerable achievements, its 1,600 workers processing some 2,600 tons of flax and 1,040 tons of tow each year.

The next owners, Oldroyd, Blakey and Latta, later M. Oldroyd & Son, used it for the manufacture of blankets, producing up to 1,000 pairs each day around 1900, when O.E. Dodgson began to manufacture blankets in part of the mills, the remainder being let out in units to Chadwick Brothers, woollen manufacturers *c.* 1930-37, Mellish, Richardson & Co., woollen manufacturers *c.* 1930-37, Cohen & Co. (later Northern Machine Screws Ltd), screw makers *c.* 1906-13, Goodby's Ltd, engineers *c.* 1910-13, William Gott,

Built in 1838 as J. Wilkinson's flax mills, Hunslet Mills are of considerable architectural and landscape value. This photograph shows them as they appeared up to the 1960s, when they fell out of use.

builders *c.* 1905-40, the Eureka Boiler Composition Co. (later Chadwick Brothers Eureka Oil Works) *c.* 1914-24, Broadhead & Conyers, leather merchants *c.* 1910-13, and William Jackson, leather merchant and boot maker *c.* 1905-18. This provides a good example of the way in which large mills were used after their original owners had gone out of business.

Dodgson's continued to weave blankets at Hunslet Mills up to 1966. In recent years the weaving sheds etc. have been demolished, and the main building has fallen into dereliction, but it is now protected as a listed building, until its future can be determined.

Just downstream from Hunslet Mills, on the other side of Goodman Street, is the site of the New Silkstone & Haigh Moor Coal Company's coal wharf, which subsequently was taken over by James Hargreaves, and since 1990 has been used by Sand & Gravel (Leeds) for landing building materials brought up the Navigation.

Continue along the footpath, past the petrol storage depots to:

116. KNOSTROP FLOOD LOCK AND THE FOOTBRIDGE

Here the channel divides into three, the first (northern) channel, which now forms the River Aire, was constructed

108

around 1900, the second channel is the Knostrop Cut, built to by-pass a circuitous section of the river under an Act of Parliament of 1774, while the third channel, which is now blocked off to form a basin, is the original course of the river, which was dammed to provide power for the early Hunslet Mills.

This footbridge over the river was erected by British Waterways, Aire and Calder Branch, in 1993 in order to enable the trail to continue down to Thwaite Mills. Funding was provided by British Waterways, Leeds City Council, and H.M. Government, through the Urban Programme.

Knostrop Flood Lock can be seen at the end of the bridge. Rebuilt in 1822, its purpose was to divert water down the river, instead of the Cut, in times of flood.

Turn left (east) here, and follow the footpath down the island between the river and the cut. On the right is:

117. BRITISH WATERWAYS KNOSTROP DEPOT

Between 1956 and 1958 British Waterways invested £230,000 to establish this depot as a modern and efficient replacement for its docks around Leeds Bridge. Its first 190ft by 120ft single-storey transit shed alone can hold up to 12,500 tons of goods.

Opposite the end of the depot, the trail crosses the site of the early 19th-century Gibraltar Leather Works, which had converted to a soap factory by the time it was demolished to make way for the new course of the river.

118. KNOSTROP LOCK

Knostrop Lock was designed to allow barges to pass between the natural course of the river and the Knostrop Cut of the late 1770s. At that period the river ran almost at right-angles to its present course, effectively preventing direct passage between the Navigation's Knostrop and Thwaite cuts.

The original lock was rebuilt in the 1820s, and became fully mechanised in 1961, when the lock-keeper's control room was erected to enable him to pass vessels through with the maximum efficiency.

119. HUNSLET RAILWAY BRIDGE

Massive stone piers here carried an enormous iron swing bridge, its length and height being required for the Navigation's plans to develop a major ship canal into Leeds. It was built by the Hunslet Railway, which was incorporated in 1893 and transferred to the Great Northern in the following year. Designed solely for freight, it left the Great Northern's Leeds-Wakefield line at Beeston Junction, then traversed an

The Hunslet Railway Bridge was built in the 1890s when there were plans to convert the Navigation into a major ship canal. In the distance, beneath the main span, is a staith for dropping coal from railway trucks into barges.

embankment to this bridge, which carried it to a terminus on the north side of the river. A connection with the North Eastern Railway's goods branch at Neville Hill then gave access to the major routes to the north-east.

The branch closed in 1967, the bridge was demolished some ten years later and its piers taken down in 1993. According to local tradition, it opened only once, and that was for testing when it was first built.

120. THWAITE LOCKS

In the improved Navigation works of the 1770s, vessels passing downstream from Leeds came down the Knostrop cut, through Knostrop Lock, then directly across the original course of the River Aire, to enter Thwaite Cut at Thwaite Locks. Although they were rebuilt as part of John Rennie's works in the early 1820s, by the 1960s the locks and their adjacent island (which was said to 'sit like a half-eaten plumb pudding in the Aire and Calder navigation') were halting the development of this major waterway. They were removed in 1967, thus allowing vessels of 500 tons or more to pass to and from Leeds.

At this point a number of early railway lines brought coal waggons down from local collieries to staiths, where the coal was shot down into boats for delivery into the town centre. They included lines from the Marchioness of Hartford's Waterloo Colliery from the 1820s, Fenton's collieries in the 1830s - 40s, and the Park, Bride and Dam pits in the 1860s.

121. KNOSTROP SEWAGE WORKS

These occupy the level ground directly to the north, across the river. During the rapid and largely unplanned expansion of early 19th-century Leeds, virtually no provision was made for the disposal of human and animal waste. As a result, many of the working-class areas were in a vile condition, the houses being engulfed by seas of excrement, 70 cartloads of it being removed from the Boot and Shoe Yard near the Kirkgate Market site in 1832. Tuberculosis, typhus, typhoid and dysentery were rife, and there were major epidemics of cholera. In 1850-55 a scheme promoted by an improvement Act of 1842 and designed by John Wignall Leather, saw the construction of the first public sewers in Leeds, all these discharging into the river here at Knostrop. Over the following years, further extensions were made, as more of the 'abominable middensteads and cesspools' were replaced by water-closets.

In 1869 a Chancery injunction prevented the corporation from discharging the raw sewage directly into the river, and so a number of contractors were employed to carry out the required purification on an experimental basis. These proved to be unacceptable, and so the first Knostrop Sewage Works were built in 1874 on the lime precipitation system. Further expansion of Leeds and its sewers rapidly outgrew this facility, and in 1907 the city was able to purchase 600 acres here, an Act of 1908 then permitting the expenditure of £1¼m on the provision of a new and efficient sewage works. Since that time, a continuous series of developments, which still continue today, have played a

Thwaite Mills are now a fascinating museum, where visitors can see a wealth of original water-powered machinery at work. When this photograph was taken in the 1950s, the Horn family were manufacturing putty and other related products here.

major part in cleaning up both the City, and, more particularly, its waterways.

122. THWAITE MILLS

A fulling mill was built at Thwaite in 1641, but the present mills and their water-wheels were erected for the Aire and Calder Navigation in 1823-5, the millwright being Thomas Hewes. The first lease was taken by W. & E. Joy, a company which specialised in crushing seeds and refining the resulting oils for lighting and lubrication. They are reputed to have made the oils for Stephenson's 'Rocket' at Thwaite Mills. For a short period both exotic dyewoods and corn were ground here too, but these were never major activities.

In 1872 the Horn family took the lease on Thwaite Mills, and adapted them for grinding flint and china stone for the local pottery industry, barytes for paint, and chalk for whitewash, putty, polish, pharmaceuticals, and even food-stuffs. By the mid-20th century their main product was putty, which continued to be manufactured up to 1976, when a flood washed away the weir, removing the mill's main source of power, and forcing it to close down.

Over the course of the next 14 years the Thwaite Mills Society, a charitable body set up to restore the mills, utilised considerable financial support from the West Yorkshire Metropolitan County Council to bring Thwaite Mills back into full working order. They are now operated by Leeds City Council as a fascinating preserved site. Here visitors can see a wealth of water-powered crushing and grinding machinery, a water-powered engineering workshop, a steam-powered crane used for unloading raw materials from boats on the Navigation, and a series of exhibitions in Thwaite House, the former home of the mills' managers. A regular series of popular events also takes place here throughout the year, as advertised in the local press.

Thwaite Mills marks the end of the Leeds Waterfront Heritage Trail. A quarter-mile walk along Thwaite Lane leads to the main Wakefield - Leeds (A61) and Pontefract - Leeds (A639) roads, with regular bus services back to the centre of Leeds.

In this part of Thwaite Mills, chalk from the 1858 crusher on the right was carried up the conveyor into the huge tommy-stones, where it was ground in water.

THE WATERWAYS CODE

Everyone who follows the Leeds Waterfront Heritage Trail, either on the towpath, or on the waterways themselves, is requested to observe the Waterways Code, to ensure that everyone enjoys their visit.

Introduction to the Code

Well over 2 million boaters, anglers, walkers and cyclists use our canals and rivers every year. With so many people using the waterways in many different ways it is important that we all get along together!

The purpose of 'The Waterways Code' is to act as a handy reference on how we can all enjoy our waterways.

The Waterways Code is supported by the following bodies:

- Inland Waterways Amenity Advisory Council

- Association of Pleasure Craft Operators

- Inland Waterways Association

- National Federation of Anglers

- British Canoe Union

- The Sports Council

- Association of Waterways Cruising Clubs

- Royal Society for the Prevention of Accidents

Courtesy on the Water

provided make certain that your mooring stakes are firmly driven in on the water side of the towing path and that they don't obstruct pedestrians.

BOATERS

• In powered craft such as cruisers or narrow boats you should keep to the centre of the channel.

• Keep your wash to a minimum by maintaining a steady speed below the allowed limit and don't slow down when passing anglers. A breaking wash created by powered boats will erode banks, harm wildlife and disturb fish.

• Avoid off-side banks - a favourite spot for anglers to catch fish. If they're given fair warning of your approach, anglers should withdraw their fishing rods.

MOORING

• Moor at recognised marked points where possible - you have priority there. Ask any anglers fishing too close to these points to move - they should be aware of the Code and oblige.

• Where an angler has established his fishing spot and there is no recognised mooring, please try and find an alternative site at least 50 ft away.

• Please don't moor opposite an angler because it will make fishing difficult.

• If mooring rings and bollards are not

POLLUTION

• Waste waters can be polluting and many forms of aquatic life and fish may be harmed. You can be fined for causing pollution from careless discharges of bilge waters

• Minimise the risks by keeping your engine in good order and soaking up excess oil using one of the absorbents generally on sale. Use biodegradable detergents for washing up.

CANOEISTS

• Paddle a careful straight course past anglers.

• When in groups keep in single file and try to avoid the off-side bank - a favourite casting spot.

• Canoes are difficult to spot, so keep a reasonable distance where you can be seen from the craft. Remember, larger craft are much less manoeuvrable and cannot use shallow water.

• Take special care when travelling through tunnels (some of which are out of bounds to canoes for safety reasons) and carry a light to make your presence known to other craft.

Courtesy on the towing path

• Take care not to block the towing path with your tackle, especially if prams, wheelchairs and bicycles are around.

• Look up your club rules or permit conditions and avoid fishing in the approaches to locks and bridges.

• Make sure you choose a site away from the outside of bends as this is where deep draughted craft need to travel.

• Stay clear of houses. Never fish near overhead powerlines (especially if you are using a carbon fibre pole).

• People aboard moored craft appreciate their privacy, so try and fish at least 50 feet away.

• A boat has priority at official mooring points - move your tackle in good time.

• When a boat approaches, raise your line well in advance and make sure the hook doesn't dangle.

BOATERS

• Use the recognised mooring rings and bollards. If none is available, hammer in stakes as close as possible to the water's edge and mark them so they are obvious to other people.

CYCLISTS

• Cycling is allowed on some towing paths. Contact the local Waterways office for details. In some cases you will need to buy a £3 permit.

• Join the towing path with care, access paths can be steep and slippery.

• Give way to other people on the towing path at all times. A 'hello' and a 'thank you' mean a lot. You must dismount and push your bicycle if the path narrows, or passes through a low bridge or alongside a lock.

• Ride at a gentle pace, in single file and do not bunch.

• Never race - you have water on one side of you.

• Take particular care on wet or uneven surfaces, and don't worsen them by skidding.

WALKERS

• Take extra care near locks and don't be tempted to assist boat crews unless you are certain of what to do.

• Remember, because boats cannot stop immediately if someone falls into the water, the risk of injury is great.

• Give anglers plenty of time to notice you and for them to move their tackle if it blocks the path.

• Ensure that you take all litter away with you, including nylon fishing lines, fish hooks, drink cans and plastic bags.

• If you have a dog make sure it is kept under close control and does not foul the towing path.

If you encounter a hazard, please notify the local Waterway Manager. The address is in your local 'phone book, or call BW Customer Services on 0923 226422.

Matches, Rallies, Events

PLANNING

• Major events play a regular and important part in the waterways' diary for every type of user. Other users should recognise the value of these activities and be prepared to make allowances.

• When organising an event, be it a boat rally, angling competition or sponsored walk, let the local Waterway Manager know at the earliest possible opportunity.

• The Manager will make sure there is no potential clash of events, advise on

procedures and how best to notify other users.

ANGLING EVENTS

• Closure of the towing path for fishing matches will be marked to make all users aware of the event.

• If you should join the towing path at an unmarked access point and find fishing in progress, please show extra consideration by respecting the requests of stewards and anglers.

• During a major angling match, mooring is permitted only at recognised points which will be clearly signposted at each end.

BOATING EVENTS

• Some towing paths may have to be closed on occasions. Any closure will be signposted well in advance. Alternative routes will normally be indicated.

• Fishing and mooring will generally not be possible whilst rallies are in progress as they use all of the available towing path.

CYCLING EVENTS

•Towing paths are not generally suitable for organised cycling events but the local Waterway Manager may give permission.

Summary of the
Code

Please:

1
Always be aware of other users.

2
Don't disturb boaters at their moorings
and anglers whilst they are fishing.

3
Keep safety in mind when fishing,
cycling, using locks and mooring your
boat.

4
Respect the canal environment and leave
the canal as you wish to find it.

5
Follow organisers' requests at events.

6
Help others to enjoy the waterways too!

British Waterways

FURTHER READING

The following books give additional information on the history and main places of interest of the Leeds Waterfront.

The Waterways

Bradley, T., *Yorkshire Rivers, The Aire, 2* (Leeds, 1893 reprinted Otley, 1988)

Clarke, M., *The Leeds and Liverpool Canal* (Ashton, 1990)

Smith, P., *The Aire and Calder Navigation* (Wakefield, 1987)

General History

Beresford, M., 'East End, West End', *Publ Thoresby Soc,* **60-61** for 1985 and 1986 (Leeds, 1988)

Brears, P., *Images of Leeds 1850-1960* (Derby, 1992)

Burt, S., *The Lord Mayor's Centenary Trails* (Leeds, 1993)

Douglas, J., Hammond, C. and Powell, K., *Leeds; Three Suburban Walks* (Leeds, 1982)

Elton, A. and Harrison, B., *Leeds in Maps* (Leeds, 1990)

Faull, M. and Moorhouse, S., *West Yorkshire: an Archaeological Survey to AD1500* (Wakefield, 1981)

Fraser, D. (ed), *A History of Modern Leeds* (Manchester, 1980)

Hatcher, J., *The Industrial Architecture of Yorkshire* (Chichester, 1985)

Heap, A. and Brears, P., *Leeds Describ'd* (Derby, 1993)

Textiles

Brears, P., *Thomas Lloyd of Armley Mills* (Wakefield, 1988)

Crump, W., 'The Leeds Woollen Industry', *Publ Thoresby Soc,* **32** for 1929 (Leeds, 1931)

Giles, C. and Goodall, I., *Yorkshire Textile Mills 1770-1930* (London, 1992)

Heaton, H., *The Yorkshire Woollen and Worsted Industries* (Oxford, 1920 reprinted 1965)

Cloth Halls and Markets

Grady, K., 'The Georgian Public Buildings of Leeds and the West Riding', *Publ Thoresby Soc,* **62** for 1987 (Leeds, 1989)

Burt, S. and Grady, K., *Kirkgate Market* (Leeds, 1992)

Industry

Anon., *Industries of Yorkshire* (London, 1888)

Anon., *The Century's Progress* (London, 1893)

Butler, R., *A History of Kirkstall Forge* (York, 1945)

Booth, A.J., *Greenwood & Batley Locomotives, 1927-1980* (Southampton, 1986)

Lackey, C., *Quality Pays. The Story of Joshua Tetley & Son* (Ascot, 1985)

Rimmer, W., 'The Leeds Leather Industry in the Nineteenth Century', *Publ Thoresby Soc,* **46** (Leeds, 1960)

Railways

Joy, D., *A Regional History of the Railways of Great Britain: South and West Yorkshire,* **38** (London, 1975)

Kirkstall Abbey

Brears, P., *Kirkstall Abbey, Leeds' Cistercian Monastery* (Leeds, 1982)

Hope, W.H. St.J. and Bilson, J., 'Architectural Description of Kirkstall Abbey', *Publ Thoresby Soc,* **16** (Leeds, 1907)

Moorhouse, S. and Wrathmell, S., 'Kirkstall Abbey Volume 1. The 1950-64 excavations: a reassessment', *Yorkshire Archaeology,* **1** (Wakefield, 1987)

Owen, D., *Kirkstall Abbey* (Leeds, *c.* 1953)

Museums

Brears, P., *Armley Mills* (Leeds, 1982)

Brears, P., *The Museum of Leeds Trail* (Leeds, 1981)

Brears, P., *Of Curiosities & Rare Things* (Leeds, 1989)

Brears, P., *Abbey House* [Information leaflet] (Leeds, 1990)

Rimmel, L., *Thwaite Mills* [Information leaflet] (Leeds, 1990)

Churches

Taylor, R., *The Ecclesia Leodienses* (London, 1875)

Savage, S. and Tyne, C., *The Labours of the Years,* [St Saviour's and St Hilda's] (Leeds, 1981)

Pollen, J., *Narrative of Five Years of St Saviour's* (Leeds, 1855)

Rusby, J., *St Peter's at Leeds* (Leeds, 1896)

USEFUL ADDRESSES

For further information on the Waterfront Heritage Trail, its major attractions, etc. please contact the relevant organisations listed below:

Leeds Tourist Information Centre
19 Wellington Street,
Leeds
LS1 4DG
(0532) 478301

Abbey House Museum
Abbey Road,
Kirkstall,
Leeds
LS5 3GH
(0532) 755821

Armley Mills Museum
Canal Road,
Armley
Leeds
LS12 2QF
(0532) 637861

British Rail Passenger Enquiries
(0532) 448133

British Trust For Conservation Volunteers
County Offices,
Hollybush Farm,
Broad Lane,
Kirkstall
Leeds
LS5 3BP
(0532) 742335

British Waterways
Aire & Calder Navigation

Lock Lane,
Castleford
West Yorkshire
WF10 2LH
(0977) 554351

British Waterways
Leeds & Liverpool Canal, East,
Dobson Lock,
Apperley Bridge,
Bradford
West Yorkshire
BD10 0PY
(0274) 611303

Eye On The Aire
Suite 2,
Salisbury Grove,
Armley,
Leeds
LS12 2AS
(0532) 319217

Granary Wharf
Arch W,
Canal Basin
Leeds
LS1 4BR
(0532) 446570

Leeds Civic Trust
17-19 Wharf Street
Leeds
LS2 7EQ
(0532) 439594

Thwaite Mills Museum
Thwaite Lane,
Stourton,
Leeds
LS10 1RP
(0532) 496453

Yorkshire Hire Cruisers Ltd
(Kirkstall Flyboat)
26 Canal Wharf,
Leeds
LS11 5PS
(0532) 456195

Acknowledgements

Leeds Waterfront and Leeds City Museums wish to record their most grateful thanks to Leeds City Council's Planning and Cultural Services committees, the National Rivers Authority and the Leeds/Bradford City Action Team for their sponsorship of this book, and the waymarking of the Trail. They also wish to thank the West Yorkshire Archaeology Service for a generous contribution towards the costs of publication.

Considerable practical help in providing the necessary information has been given by the staff of the Leeds Local History Library, especially Mrs A. Heap, by Mr D. Sheard, the City Libraries' photographer, Mr D. Blackburn of British Waterways, Mr S. Burt, Mr K. Grady, Director of Leeds Civic Trust, Mr P. Kelley and Mr G. Horsman of Armley Mills, Mr P. Larkin of Abbey House, Mr N. Dolan of Thwaite Mills, The Royal Armouries, and by no means least, Mr D. Waterman, Director of Leeds Waterfront.

Sincere thanks are also due to Mrs G. Philipson of the City Museum for typing the manuscript, and to the following members of staff from the West Yorkshire Archaeology Service: Ms S. Frankland for designing the booklet, Mrs M. Schofield and Mrs A. Whawell for typing the text onto disk, Mrs P. White for typesetting and design, Ms C. Philo for sub-editing, Mr J. Prudhoe and Mr A. Swann for additional illustrations and Mr P. Gwilliam for additional photography.